Bradley

The Great Generals Series

This distinguished new series features the lives of eminent military leaders who changed history in the United States and abroad. Top military historians write concise but comprehensive biographies including the personal lives, battles, strategies, and legacies of these great generals, with the aim to provide background and insight into today's armies and wars. These books are of interest to the military history buff, and, thanks to fast-paced narratives and references to current affairs, they are also accessible to the general reader.

Patton by Alan Axelrod

Grant by John Mosier

Eisenhower by John Wukovits

LeMay by Barrett Tillman

MacArthur by Richard B. Frank

Stonewall Jackson by Donald A. Davis

Pershing by James Lacey

Andrew Jackson by Robert Remini

Bradley

Alan Axelrod

First published in 2008 by
PALGRAVE MACMILLAN™
175 Fifth Avenue, New York, N.Y. 10010 and
Houndmills, Basingstoke, Hampshire, England RG21 6XS.
Companies and representatives throughout the world.

PALGRAVE MACMILLAN is the global academic imprint of the Palgrave Macmillan division of St. Martin's Press, LLC and of Palgrave Macmillan Ltd. Macmillan® is a registered trademark in the United States, United Kingdom and other countries. Palgrave is a registered trademark in the European Union and other countries.

ISBN-13: 978-0-230-60018-8
ISBN-10: 0-230-60018-2

Library of Congress Cataloging-in-Publication Data is available from the Library of Congress.

A catalogue record of the book is available from the British Library.

Design by Letra Libre

First edition: January 2008

10   9   8   7   6   5   4   3   2   1

Printed in the United States of America.

Contents

Photosection appears between pages 106 and 107.

Foreword

Understanding Omar Bradley, America's top ground commander in World War II Europe, is key to understanding the character, strengths, and institutional weaknesses of the United States Army. Unassuming, of humble roots, a teacher by temperament, Bradley held all the big jobs during and immediately after the war—Corps Commander, Army Commander, Army Group Commander, Army Chief of Staff, and first Chairman of the Joint Chiefs of Staff. No one left a greater imprint on the style and substance of the Army over a period of almost sixty years. Yet he has remained unappreciated. Alan Axelrod's fast-moving biography brings Bradley's character and contribution to life for a new generation of Americans, and helps us understand the foundation of today's Army.

Bradley's father was a schoolteacher and a coach. Growing up in nineteenth-century America, Bradley often walked with his father to school together, a miles-long trip. His father died early, and his mother took in boarders and did laundry to support the family. Bradley went to work for a railroad after high school. For him, West Point was little more than a paid education and a further chance to participate in sports. Not surprisingly, he wasn't high on "flash and dash." Instead he exhibited steady competence, teamwork, and loyalty. Yet as Axelrod shows, he had the wit to work with and use Patton, however much he distrusted elements of Patton's flashing, dashing temperament.

His significance as a combat leader in World War II is difficult to overstate. He participated in almost all the critical actions and decisions in North Africa and Europe, from the cleanup after the American defeat at Kasserine Pass in early 1943, through the invasion of Sicily, the planning for the cross-Channel invasion, D-Day, the breakout of the beachheads, the race through France, the dark days of the Battle of the Bulge, and the final push into Germany. He—not Eisenhower—was the American counterpoint to British Field Marshal Montgomery. It was Bradley's common sense, resistance to self-aggrandizing publicity, personal hard work, commitment to teamwork, and low-key temperament that won him the affection of his soldiers and the continued support of his military superiors. Relatively speaking, Omar Bradley was probably the "lowest maintenance" of any of the top World War II personalities.

His enduring legacy among the American military and his long-term institutional impact rested heavily on this command personality. Again and again, in the post–World War II period, the Army as an institution has worked to identify and promote the kind of leader Bradley was: low-key, substantive, solid, loyal, and practical. Leaders in the Bradley mold repress or contain their personal insecurities and idiosyncrasies, abjure the florid personalities, overt militarism, and preening that civilians have traditionally associated with military high-command, and patiently do their part for the team effort. As subordinates, they act thoughtfully and tactfully present their ideas, and work to gain the loyalty and personal regard of their bosses. They work harmoniously with colleagues and, within their command, teach, explain, and support the decisions of their leaders. They are "organization men," not "Einsteins." They aim not to "stand out" but to "keep standing in." They are survivors. And for its own survival and effectiveness the Army and other large organizations need leaders like Omar Bradley.

General Omar Bradley reorganized the Army staff, and organized the Joint Chiefs of Staff. Perhaps he believed he was following the pattern set by his mentor, George C. Marshall, but it was Bradley who set the operating system and the operating style that provided the basis for the modern military-industrial complex. He also picked the leadership. It was Bradley, his subordinates, and their subordinates who really set the tone for much that the Army was to become during the Korean War era, and even in the post–Vietnam era. It was Bradley's image and influence as a teacher, team builder, coach, and loyal, selfless leader that has inspired generation after generation of Army leaders in countless ways. For example, in the Army, leadership often expresses a desire to "have a strong bench." Or in the warnings, repeated year after year to newly selected Brigadier Generals that they are collectively no better and no different than the fifty Colonels who just missed the selection. Even today, as the Army puts unprecedented effort into protecting each individual soldier, it can take its inspiration from Omar Bradley, who put great emphasis on understanding and looking after the welfare of the men he commanded.

Yet there is another side of Bradley, a side that is also part of the Army legacy that he gave us. Bradley was the anti-Patton, the advocate of big firepower and logistics, not bold maneuver, the advocate of "broad front" rather than daring thrust, the advocate of prudence—caution— not risk-taking; the advocate for the common man, rather than for military "genius." There was a lore about Bradley among some who knew him, a reputation that lurked beneath the favorable public images. I heard it first from a retired general who, as a lieutenant, had heard Bradley veto MacArthur's daring plan for an amphibious invasion at Inchon. Bradley then was outmaneuvered bureaucratically by MacArthur, and the operation succeeded brilliantly, while Bradley, angered, waited, supported, and probably encouraged MacArthur's eventual relief by President Truman. I heard the criticisms again from another retired four-star, who as a Brigadier General, was a key combat leader in the Battle of the Bulge. "When Ike relieved Brad . . ." he began, as he was explaining his own leadership philosophy. "Excuse me, Sir, but General Bradley was relieved?" I asked. "Out of touch. Too cautious," he answered. "Of course, Ike couldn't actually replace him because of the political sensitivities." However, there has always been this undertone about Bradley among some of the officers who knew him or served with him.

No one rises to high military command without enormous talent, skills, and dedication. None of the generals in this series are normal, average, or ordinary. Yet how much room is there inside the armed forces for innovation, risk taking, speaking up to the boss, and the kind of charismatic leadership that can move armies? And what are the consequences if the answer is, "Not much"? In the tragic aftermath of the costly intervention in Iraq, these are questions that must be asked. Alan Axelrod's biography of Omar Nelson Bradley helps us ask and answer these questions.

—General Wesley K. Clark

Introduction

The best reporters follow the best leads, and the best leads typically come from the very top. When the top commander in North Africa, Ike Eisenhower, advised America's most popular war correspondent, Ernie Pyle, to "go discover Bradley," he did not have to be told twice, although it took a little while. Pyle did not catch up with Bradley until the end of the Sicily campaign, but then he stuck with Bradley "like a shadow for three days" and produced a six-part newspaper feature avidly followed in the States.[1] For better or worse, the legend of the "GI General" was born.

For better or worse, too, the wartime American public required a set of ready hooks on which to hang their hero worship. Thus Americans learned to regard George C. Marshall as the quiet brains behind the war effort. Dwight D. "Ike" Eisenhower was the supremely confident and charismatic supreme Allied commander. Bernard Law Montgomery was the best of the Brits, conqueror of the best of the Germans, the "Desert Fox" Erwin Rommel. In the Pacific, Douglas MacArthur ran the whole show and was America's Caesar. Among the U.S. field commanders, George S. Patton Jr. was, of course, the most famous, infamous, and generally colorful—a headline grabber if there ever was one. But until Ernie Pyle publicized him, Omar Nelson Bradley had no public profile at all. After Pyle's "GI General" angle supplied the missing hook, Bradley finally entered into a prominence that his burgeoning responsibilities—from II

Corps commander in North Africa to Twelfth U.S. Army Group commander in Europe, leader of 1.3 million men—surely merited.

Thus elevated in the public imagination, and despite a nearly career-wrecking tactical lapse in the Battle of the Bulge and a potentially damning role in Ike's controversial strategic decision to concede Berlin to the Soviet Red Army, Omar Bradley ended World War II as a well-loved popular hero. His very lack of glamour, his homely looks, his ordinary GI uniforms, his soft-spoken command presence, his demonstrated concern for the welfare of his troops, his evident common sense, and his humble Missouri origin made him the antithesis of his most famous subordinate, Patton. Although many Americans recognized that Patton had performed magnificently in war, they were uncomfortable with him, and rightly so. Arrogant and aristocratic—sufficiently brutal to have slapped a pair of soldiers suffering from battle fatigue—to many he seemed more Prussian than American. Bradley, in contrast, appeared to be the ideal soldier-officer of a democratic nation.

In the years since World War II, however, the controversy surrounding Patton has faded, and his star has risen, thanks in no small measure to the iconic 1970 film biography, *Patton,* with George C. Scott in the title role. During those same years, Bradley has not so much faded from the public consciousness as his significance has become vague. Beyond his deep concern for his men, what, exactly, did he do? Patton is a legend. Omar Bradley is not.

Worse for the Bradley legacy, military historians as well as military history buffs have tended to be increasingly critical of his generalship. His methodical approach to operations was, at times, overly cautious, allowing tactical and even strategic opportunities to slip away; he was more of a gambler than Montgomery, but far less of one than Patton. And, of course, his willingness to leave the Ardennes thinly defended in December 1944 brought on the surprise German offensive that was the Battle of the Bulge, an encounter that cost the Americans—seemingly on the verge of victory in Europe—more heavily than any other battle in the European theater.

Some recent military historians point out that Bradley was neither a bold field commander, like Patton, nor a top strategist, like Eisenhower, but, rather, occupied a layer of command between these extremes, essentially ensuring that someone else's strategy was carried out in the field by others. Other military historians, such as Charles Whiting, believe that in the culminating months and weeks of the European command, Bradley took a very significant role in creating original strategy—but this view has not necessarily raised Bradley in historical estimation.[2]

Of the major American figures of World War II, Bradley is the only one whose public postwar career was mainly in the military. Patton succumbed to injuries sustained in a car wreck in December 1946, which cut short his postwar career; Marshall became a distinguished statesman, emissary to China, advocate of the "Marshall Plan," secretary of state, and secretary of defense; and Eisenhower served as army chief of staff and as supreme Allied commander of the North Atlantic Treaty Organization (NATO), his postwar career was chiefly defined by his two terms as president of the United States. Bradley, in contrast, after the war served as the vigorously reform-minded director of the Veterans Administration, then army chief of staff, first chairman of the Joint Chiefs of Staff (JCS), and chair of NATO's military committee as well as the inner-circle "standing group" within that committee. He did not shape Cold War policy, but he advised on it, and he managed much of its military execution. He was, perhaps, the first American military commander called upon to think and work in genuinely global terms. Yet when he stepped down as JCS chairman and also relinquished his NATO posts, Bradley took a position in the private sector and faded from the American military scene through the nearly three decades of life left to him.

Bradley wrote—or, more accurately, collaborated on—a memoir and an autobiography. *A Soldier's Story* (1951) brilliantly narrates his experience in World War II, but was in large part the work of his longtime aide Chet Hansen, who virtually ghosted the volume. *A General's Life* (published posthumously in 1983) is a full-scale autobiography, written in collaboration with journalist Clay Blair, who fashioned the volume from taped interview sessions supplemented by full access to Bradley's papers.

Surprisingly, no full-length biography of Omar Bradley exists, and while the present study, of modest length, makes no claim to being such a biography, its aim is nevertheless to present an objective narrative of the general's life, including a just evaluation of his enduring significance to American military history.

Let us concede that the most durable aspect of Bradley's popular image, that of the "GI General," was invented by Ernie Pyle. Yet let us also recognize that he did not fabricate it out of whole cloth. The form and the substance were there. Like Ike Eisenhower, Bradley sprang from humble roots in the American hinterland. Like Eisenhower, he never wholly severed his connection to those roots. And also as with Eisenhower, the story of Bradley's rise within the army and onto the world stage is the more remarkable for the humble, unassuming character and homely, salt-of-the-earth values of the man. Bradley saw army life—and he saw war—from the dual perspectives of the ordinary soldier (the man he liked to call the "doughboy") and the top levels of planning and command. He never lost that twin focus. If Patton wove dreams of glory, Bradley focused first on dishwater-dull logistics and commonsense matters of morale. Only after these were taken care of did he draw up his tactical plans. As Ernie Pyle saw it, that did not make him overly cautious or unimaginative; it made him a GI General.

At this remove in time from World War II, it is easy to dismiss Pyle's creation. But to do so would be wrong. Superficial though it may be, it points to the very source of Omar Nelson Bradley's enduring significance for today's military leaders. Bradley was—and endures as—a model of the American commander of a democratic army fighting to defend the values of a democracy.

CHAPTER 1

Missouri Boy

When he was 25, John Smith Bradley, a teacher at the Fairview School near Higbee, Missouri, fell in love with one his pupils, 16-year-old Sarah Elizabeth Hubbard. He married her on May 12, 1892, and, nine months later—to the day—Omar Nelson Bradley was born. It was, Bradley pointed out in his autobiography, Lincoln's birthday. He did not presume to push the coincidence of dates too far, but he did observe that he was born in the very place in which his parents had been married, the home of the Hubbards, "a crude three-room log house."[1]

The point Bradley wanted to make was not that he was a second Lincoln, but that, like Lincoln, he was a rural Midwesterner, a boy of most humble origin who would rise to singular prominence. The point, in fact, was less about Lincoln or Bradley than it was about America, because only in America could boys such as these rise to prominence in the service of their country. The point was also about roots, about sturdy stock, about character, about good, noble, hard qualities that seemed to grow from the very soil of the heartland.

George Smith Patton Jr., who would serve with Bradley first as his senior and then as his subordinate, reveled in the role of spiritual heir to romantic Revolutionary and Civil War commanders, all chivalrous, well-heeled, and nobly self-sacrificing, whereas Bradley celebrated the grit and poverty of his decidedly common ancestors.

The Bradleys had come to Madison County, Kentucky, from the British Isles during the mid-1700s, then moved early in the nineteenth century to what would become Missouri, settling on small farms in the middle part of the state, near the agricultural village of Clark and the coal-mining town of Higbee. Bradley's grandfather, Thomas Minter Bradley, was a Confederate private who, after the war, married Sarah Elizabeth Lewis, daughter of a poor Clark farmer, and raised nine children, of whom the future general's father, born February 15, 1867, was the oldest. Sarah Elizabeth Hubbard, Omar Bradley's mother, called Bessie, came from a poor farming family in Clark, a background almost identical to that of her husband, except that her father had served in the Union Army.

John Smith Bradley was "the first Bradley to break out of the mold." He started out like everybody else, a sodbuster, but, after educating himself as far as he could, he enrolled in a local school and emerged just two years later qualified as a rural schoolteacher. "My father was a curious blend of frontiersman, sportsman, farmer and intellectual," Omar Bradley proudly observed. He was "powerfully built and fearless," the best marksman in Randolph County, who became a rural "pioneer in baseball," carving his own bats, teaching himself the art of the curve ball, and organizing a series of local teams—on which he was always the stand-out player. During the school year he taught, and in the summer he worked as a farmhand or sharecropper, but, whatever season, he always found time to read and to pass on his love of books to his family as well as to his students.[2]

The portrait Bradley painted of his father was not larger than life. It was, rather, life size. Bradley saw his father as an extraordinary ordinary man. Molded of the Missouri soil, he broke out of the mold, and, in doing so, created the very mold from which his son was struck: a small-town athlete, a crack shot for whom baseball became a passion, a keen student, a soldier, a teacher of soldiers, and a leader of soldiers. Abraham Lincoln traveled far beyond his Kentucky and Illinois roots, but it is a key to the truth of the Lincoln mythology that he never really left those roots behind. So, too, with Bradley, whose career would take him a long way from rural Missouri, but not so far that he ever really left it behind. His first name may have evoked the *Rubaiyat of Omar Khayyam,* the exotic book of Persian verse universally popular in Victorian England and America via Edward Fitzgerald's translation, and his middle name Lord Horatio Nelson, the victor of Trafalgar. But they had, in truth, the homeliest of origins. Omar D. Gray was a local newspaper editor John Smith Bradley admired, and Nelson was "the name of a local doctor."[3]

Before he turned four, Omar made way for two new additions to his family, seven-year-old Nettie and six-year-old Opal, the daughters of his mother's older sister, who succumbed to tuberculosis. In February 1900, when Omar was seven, Bessie Bradley gave birth to another boy of her own, Raymond Clavert, who died of scarlet fever just days before his second birthday.

Although Omar Bradley's youthful world was local, concentrated in and around Higbee, it was also peripatetic. As his father moved from one rural school to another, so Omar moved from school to school, and because the Bradleys could not afford a horse and buggy, he and his father walked to and from the classroom every day, father setting "a hearty pace—seventeen minutes to the mile." It was ideal preparation for military marching.[4]

With the physical conditioning of a rigorous life lived largely on foot came a growth of mind and emotion. Omar often found the long march to and from school hard, but he relished the hours spent alone with his father, regarding them as an early lesson in leadership and morale. He learned to read very quickly, his father teaching him to devour books, especially history, and in particular accounts of the French and Indian War, the American Revolution, and the Civil War. Omar would act out whatever battle he read about, using dominoes to build forts on the parlor rug, hollow elderberry reeds for artillery, and empty .22 cartridges to represent soldiers.

Omar Bradley had no shortage of "soldiers." Empty cartridges abounded in the Bradley household, as his father was an expert marksman with a .22 rifle as well as with a 12-gauge shotgun, which he used to bag "almost all the meat mother put on the table." John Smith Bradley gave his son a pump-action BB rifle when he turned six. The boy accompanied his father on hunting trips, and although he could not kill any game with a BB rifle, he learned how to walk with a hunter's stealth, and he learned how to handle a rifle competently, confidently, and safely. Off on his own, he would shoot frogs, which he contributed to the family's meals. Later, when Mr. Bradley presented his son with a Stevens .22 rifle, the boy felt he had achieved manhood. Yet it came with a lesson in humility. "I saw a squirrel in the top of a tree and signaled to my father. He went to the opposite side of the tree, forcing the squirrel to my side. As carefully as I knew how, I shot three times. The squirrel never moved." The senior Bradley examined the rifle and, discovering that the sights were out of line, he adjusted them, raised the weapon to his shoulder, turned to his son, and announced, "If I don't knock his eye out, something is very wrong with the sights." With that, he planted a single shot in the animal's right eye. "That was the last time I ever fired a rifle with the sights out of line," Bradley recalled.[5] Firearms became a way of life for Omar Bradley, as important and as real as books.

When he was 12, the Bradleys moved into the town of Higbee itself so that Omar could attend the public school there. This meant that Mr. Bradley had to walk as much as seven miles each day, every day, to and from the rural schools in which he taught. To help pay for the house Mr. Bradley purchased at a sheriff's sale, Omar, his mother, Nettie, and Opal added to the family income by taking turns operating a switchboard for a 90-telephone rural system. The boy deeply appreciated the sacrifices that were being made to educate him, and he excelled at his classes in Higbee, earning in his first year a 94 grade point average that put him at the head of his class.

Study and shooting were not all that consumed the young man's life. He imbibed from his father a third passion, baseball, which swallowed up summer after summer. And always in the background—distinctly in the background—were two more pastimes: religion and politics. John Smith Bradley had been raised in the Church of Christ, Bessie Hubbard in the

Baptist Church. After marriage, she converted, and the Bradleys worshipped every Sunday at the local Church of Christ. As for politics, the family was naturally Populist, siding with the likes of William Jennings Bryan and against the "big trusts" and the "robber barons."

The life into which Omar Nelson Bradley grew was as hard as it was simple, but it was leavened by the satisfaction of achievements in school, on the hunt, and on the baseball diamond and not least by the camaraderie of a loving family—of a loving mother, of cousins who were really adoptive sisters, and most of all, of a father, a stern, strong, yet gentle model of manhood whom young Bradley unabashedly "idolized."[6]

At the end of the school year in 1907, Omar Bradley's average grade was 98.66, putting him again at the top of the class. But the winter of 1907–1908 was very hard, and it was especially hard on John Smith Bradley, who walked a six-mile round trip to Ebenezer School and came home one January evening deathly ill. Pneumonia, the doctor said. He took to his bed, a few days passed, and at four o'clock on a morning two weeks before his forty-first birthday, Omar Bradley's father died.

The *Higbee Weekly News* mourned: "No better citizen ever lived among us." And it celebrated: "The world is better for his having lived in it, and although he is gone from among us, his life was such that it will have influence for good years to come." In these words printed about the end of his father's life, there was for Omar a lesson about the purpose of life—though, doubtless, the fifteen-year-old was himself too sick (he had a bad cold the day his father died) and too shattered to take it in immediately. He would soon appreciate the legacy left to him, which lay not in a heavily mortgaged house, but in a determination to continue his education, to make something of himself, to love the outdoors, and to embrace a catalog of homely, noble virtues, a list anyone destined to serve with or under General Bradley would have recognized as perfectly characteristic of him: "A sense of justice and respect. . . . Integrity. Sobriety. Patriotism. Religiosity."[7]

+≻━≺+

If the death of his father diminished Omar Bradley's world, it also broadened it. Unable to carry the mortgage payments on the Higbee house,

Bessie Bradley rented it out and moved the family to Moberly, which Bradley described as "a big new city about fifteen miles north, home of the Wabash Railroad and the Brown Shoe Company." She rented a house on the city's South Fourth Street, took in two boarders, and set up as a professional seamstress. Omar earned a little money delivering the *Moberly Democrat* and enrolled in Moberly High School, whose administration, apparently unimpressed by his outstanding record in a rural school, admitted Omar as a sophomore instead of a junior. Undaunted, the young man threw himself into sports as well as academics, joining informally organized track and baseball teams and becoming a self-confessed baseball nut.[8]

In addition to high school, Omar attended the Sunday school of Central Christian Church. Classes were taught by Eudora Quayle, a widow with two teenage daughters, Sarah Jane and Mary Elizabeth, the former two years younger than Omar and the latter six months older than he. That turned out to be a problem, because Omar Bradley was instantly drawn to wide-eyed, petite Mary, but, since he had been put back a year, she was in the junior class ahead of him. Moreover, she was already being squired about by an older boy, who had already graduated. Quiet and shy, Omar was reticent around girls, perhaps self-conscious about his awkward, gangly looks, long arms, huge hands, and heavy jaw. He did not date Mary, or anyone else, the whole time he was in high school, but through his faithful attendance at Sunday school and church, he "came to know all the Quayle women quite well."[9]

In the fall of 1909, he began his junior year at Moberly High, but, at midterm, school authorities suddenly reversed their earlier decision to hold him back, and Omar found himself catapulted from the class of 1911 into the senior class of 1910. It was Mary Quayle's class—and yet Omar never felt that he was accepted by her classmates, "a closely knit, clannish group that had been together since grammar school days." Except for his baseball team mates and Mary herself, Omar "did not get to know any of them well . . . and remained the 'loner' or 'outsider' from Higbee."[10]

Shy, awkward, fatherless, and lonely, Omar met with what he called "an absolutely catastrophic accident" in the winter of 1909 while skating on a frozen lake in a city park at night. He collided with another skater, smashing his teeth against the other boy's head, knocking most of them loose and damaging his gums. Because he knew that his family could not afford to send him to a dental surgeon, Bradley suffered in silence. For years thereafter, his teeth and gums were a source of trouble and pain, both physical and emotional. "I never smiled when my picture was taken, but rather closed my lips tightly to avoid there being any permanent record of that jumbled mess."[11]

When he graduated in 1910, Bradley's Moberly grades were somewhat lower than they had been in Higbee: grades of 96 and 94 in science and math, respectively, and 90 and 85 in English and history, making a cumulative GPA of 91.4. For no reason Bradley himself could fathom, the editors of the school yearbook placed his senior picture alongside that of Mary Quayle.

Graduation left open the question of career. Curiously enough, the reticent Bradley, significantly better in math than in English, decided on a career in law, but, without enough money to go to college, and reluctant to deprive his mother of his help, he decided to return full time for a year to a job he had held part time during the summer. He hired on as a laborer in the locomotive shops of the Wabash Railroad, first in the supply department and then in the higher-paying boiler shop, where he earned 17 cents an hour, 9 hours a day, 6 days a week.

Putting off college was not the only hardship Bradley endured after graduation. Mary Quayle left for classes at the State Normal School in far-off St. Cloud, Minnesota, where her aunt was on the faculty. Mary planned to spend two years there in the hope that her family's finances, only marginally better than those of the Bradleys, would permit her transfer to the University of Missouri. Omar would see little of her for the next several years. In the meantime, however, Bessie Bradley—who was now only 35—met John Robert "Bob" Maddox, "a poor farmer, very hard of hearing," recently widowed and left with a two-year-old and a seven-year-old son to care for. Bessie married Maddox on Christmas Day 1910, he and the boys moved into the South Fourth Street house, the boarders moved out, and Bessie Bradley let the Higbee house go to sheriff's auction, where its sale price of $441.20 satisfied the mortgage. With that financial burden lifted and with a man in the house, Omar now felt free to enter the University of Missouri in the fall of 1911. He would study to become a lawyer.

So the matter was settled—until a conversation one day with John Cruson, the local Sunday school superintendent.

"Why don't you try for West Point?" Cruson casually suggested.

Young Bradley had read enough history to make the name familiar, but he had also read enough to respond almost mechanically: "I couldn't afford West Point." [12]

Perhaps amused by the young man's naïveté, Cruson assured him that not only was the academy free, but that, wonder of wonders, cadets were even paid a modest stipend while they attended.

For Omar Bradley, West Point was at this juncture neither more nor less than a free education—even better, an education that paid a little something. This was enough to send him talking to his mother, who was at first reluctant to allow her son to try out for the academy. Unlike the pacifist Mennonite mother of another West Point hopeful, a Kansas boy named Dwight David Eisenhower (he, too, aspired to join the class of 1915), Bessie Bradley's objections were not based on religion conviction. The prospect of her son training to become a warrior and a leader of warriors did not bother her nearly so much as the fact that West Point was a very long way from Moberly. Omar prevailed, however, and composed a longhand letter to his congressman, soliciting nomination as a cadet.

CHAPTER 2

Runner Up

Congressman William M. Rucker responded promptly to Omar Bradley's letter requesting nomination to West Point. At the time, each of the nation's congressmen and senators was permitted to nominate one West Point cadet every four years. Rucker's reply explained that his current nominee was in his third year at the academy, so it would be a full year before Bradley could apply—and even then, of course, there would be no promises. Other candidates appealing to Rucker might be more qualified.

A full year—that seemed to settle the matter once and for all. Bradley again decided to apply to the University of Missouri. But then Congress intervened, voting, in the spring of 1911, to amend the law so that representatives and senators could appoint a cadet every three years. Accordingly, on June 27, Bradley received another letter from Representative Rucker. The good news was that the law had changed; the bad was that Rucker had already nominated one Dempsey Anderson, a boy from his hometown of Keytesville. By way of consolation, Rucker offered

Bradley the dubious honor of becoming his alternate candidate. He would take the same physical and academic examinations Anderson took, and if Anderson happened to fail but Bradley happened to pass, the nomination would go to him.

Rucker's letter reached Bradley just eight days before the examinations were scheduled to be given, at Jefferson Barracks, St. Louis, on July 5. After his conversation with Sunday school superintendent Cruson, Bradley had sent away for literature on West Point, and he knew that the tests would cover geography, geometry, algebra, and—what he most dreaded—English. He faced a dilemma. Working in the locomotive shop, he had been out of school and away from blackboards and textbooks for a year. As for algebra, that was a subject he'd last given thought to three years earlier, back in provincial Higbee. He could quit the Wabash Railroad to cram full time for the exam, but that, he concluded, "seemed imprudent." This left the option of nocturnal study, "after a long hard day's work in the boiler shop." Even at that, he had only a few days, whereas he figured that Dempsey Anderson had been preparing for a long time. "It seemed foolish to spend hard-earned, much-needed money on a round-trip ticket to St. Louis with the odds stacked so heavily against me."[1]

Bradley's attitude toward the exam was predictive of his later approach to strategy and tactics. He valued prudence above practically all else, but he invariably knew when to start pushing the envelope. For he would never make the mistake of equating prudence with paralysis. Even with the odds stacked against him, Bradley did not give up on West Point out of hand. Instead, he sought the advice of the superintendent of Moberly schools, J. C. Lilly, a friend of his father's. Lilly listened, weighed the pros and cons, then advised Bradley to try for it. Even if he failed, Lilly counseled, the experience would be worthwhile. Still, Bradley balked, reluctant to lose paying work time and to lay out cash for a train ticket. He decided that only if the railroad would give him both time off *and* a free pass to St. Louis would he take the exam. His employer generously did both of those things.

———

It was Omar Bradley's first trip to a big city, but he took no time for sightseeing, instead furiously cramming on the streetcar to Jefferson Barracks, where he found himself in a room with a dozen other candidates and alternate candidates. He met Dempsey Anderson, whose father had been the Keytesville sheriff and a good friend of Rucker. Not only was the young man a year older than Bradley, he had been studying a full year for the exams. Bradley's heart sank.

The exams consumed a grueling four days, one day per subject area, four hours each day. Algebra, not English, proved to be the real bear. After two hours, Bradley had solved less than a third of the minimum number of problems necessary to pass. Surrender seemed the prudent choice, and so, discouraged and angry at having come all the way to St. Louis, he gathered his papers and walked up to the proctor, intending to turn them in and return to Moberly and the locomotive shop. That was that.

But when he approached the officer who served as proctor, he observed that the man was so deeply engrossed in a book that it simply seemed impolite to disturb him. For that reason—and apparently for that reason alone—Bradley returned to his desk, resolved to give it another try. As if by magic, no sooner did he sit down again than theorems learned three years earlier rushed back to him, and Bradley settled back to work with a passion, completing a little more than the required 67 percent of the problems by the end of the allotted four hours. Encouraged, he returned for the rest of the exams, which he found so tough that, when the four days were done, he returned to Moberly with the absolute certainty that he would never go to West Point.

On July 27, a telegram arrived informing Omar Nelson Bradley that he had been appointed to West Point, to which he was to report before noon on August 1.

His initial response was not joy, but the firm conviction that a mistake had been made. He did a most unusual thing for any resident of Moberly, let alone a poor Bradley. He picked up the telephone and called Dempsey Anderson 30 miles away in Keytesville. No, Anderson told him, there was no mistake. He himself had just received a telegram announcing that he had failed. Two days after this exchange, a letter arrived from Congressman Rucker, congratulating Bradley and blandly pointing out that he had made the "required grade" in each exam, whereas Anderson had failed "some." Even now, however, Bradley remained reticent, burdened by a feeling of guilt, as if he had stolen Anderson's opportunity.

He telephoned Anderson, offering to decline the appointment in the expectation that Anderson might thereby regain it. But the youth manfully demurred: "You have won," he said.[2]

+⟞⟝+

The afternoon of July 30 found Omar Bradley—alone—on the worn wooden platform of the Moberly Wabash station. A small suitcase was at his feet, most of his clothes having been shipped ahead to West Point in a steamer trunk. Into his pocket was crammed all of his money, one hundred dollars. At the end of a 24-hour ride, he was at the station of Highland Falls, New York, the Hudson River village that lay just outside the gate of the United States Military Academy. He spent the night in the local hotel, awoke early, and, before noon (as ordered), presented himself to the sergeant on duty.

For George S. Patton Jr., West Point had meant and would always mean just one thing: the first phase in the fulfillment of what he knew to be his military "destiny." For Bradley, West Point was not so much the portal into a military destiny as an ideal place for a "young boy who had lost his father and might have unconsciously been in search of a surrogate." As Bradley saw it, West Point was a veritable repository of strong father figures. It was also perfect for a boy who loved math, science, and sports—especially sports. Star athletes, he soon understood, were also the stars of the Corps of Cadets.[3]

The society that was the Corps of Cadets in 1911 was a small one. Total enrollment at West Point that year consisted of just 600 cadets, of whom 265 were "plebes"—West Point terminology for freshmen. Yet even in this small and select group, Bradley managed to feel like an outsider. The majority had been accepted in the spring and had reported early to a pre-semester summer camp on June 14. Bradley was among 14 cadets who, because of the last-minute change in the law, reported late, thereby missing the first 7 weeks of the summer camp. This stigmatized him (along with the other 13) as an "Augustine"—he had reported in August—because the other cadets resented that he (and the others) had missed out on 7 weeks of hazing (called "crawling") in so-called beast barracks. Bradley believed that even the administration and faculty held his group's involuntary tardiness against them, since neither Bradley nor the others were promoted to cadet officer or noncom ranks until they became first classmen (seniors).

But Bradley did not complain. Nor did he complain about the roommate he drew: a "lackadaisical Southerner" named Benjamin W. Mills, who was "not too bright" and who, against all the rules, smoked throughout his four years at the academy. "Had I not spent countless hours coaching him in math and science, Bennie Mills would not have made it through his first year." Even the hazing (as it turned out, the Corps had plenty to spare, even after the first seven weeks Bradley had missed) had its positive aspects for Bradley, who wrote that it "impressed upon us the sense of rank and privilege and taught us to unquestioningly obey orders, fundamental grounding for any soldier." In the much-dreaded system of demerits—or "skins"—that the academy traditionally used to enforce discipline, Bradley was also able to find laudable virtue. Each cadet was allowed nine demerits per month. Any earned beyond this had to be "walked off" by marching back and forth with a rifle, one hour for each demerit—"a humiliating—and boring—punishment." When Bradley accumulated 16 demerits his first month, he found that walking off his 7 hours "had the desired effect on me. Thereafter I remained well below the allowable nine demerits."[4]

At the time, Bradley knew he had ample reason for refraining from complaint. A poor boy from the sticks, he was getting what he considered a world-class education for free. And in retrospect, there was even less to complain about. Bradley's class, the Class of 1915, would be immortalized in the annals of the academy as "the Class the Stars Fell on." Of 265 incoming cadets, 59 would become generals, and of them, Dwight D. Eisenhower and Bradley would rise to five-star rank.

For the balance of the "summer camp" that preceded the fall semester proper, Bradley reveled in the hiking, tent living, and—most of all—the target practice, for which his father's hunting and rifle lessons proved perfect preparation. He also found pleasure and fulfillment in sports, especially in his beloved baseball. One afternoon, the West Point baseball coach, Sam Strang Nicklin, formerly a New York Giant, watched Bradley and the other plebes play. Playing left field, Bradley got in some good long throws to home plate and, as a batter, hit a home run. Nicklin approached Bradley after the game and told him that one of his home plate throws was the longest he had ever seen. Jotting down on a card bearing Bradley's name and class, "Bats right, throws right, hits curve, fine arm," Nicklin indicated that he might join the varsity team in the spring of 1912.[5]

Academically, Bradley did not start off nearly so auspiciously. His grades on the Jefferson Barracks tests were passing, but not much better than that. In the academy of Bradley's student days, cadets were grouped into 12-man sections numbered 1 through 28. Those with the best grades were put into Section 1, those with the worst (who were called "goats") were consigned to Section 28. Bradley began in Section 24 in math and Section 27 in history and English. He worked hard to get out of goat territory, however, and by the end of his plebe year stood number 49 in his 265-cadet class.

As Nicklin had all but promised, Cadet Bradley made the varsity baseball squad in the spring. Although he was not put on the first team, his mere presence on the squad instantly elevated him in West Point society. Not only did he earn recognition from upperclassmen, he was welcomed into Omicron Pi Phi, a secret and illegal fraternity (absolutely banned some years after Bradley had graduated) made up almost exclusively of top athletes. By his sophomore year, Cadet Bradley also made the junior varsity football team.

The Class of 1915 was given its first summer furlough in 1913, during which Bradley played semi-pro baseball with the Moberly team (refusing pay so as not to compromise his West Point baseball eligibility) and began dating Mary Quayle, who, having graduated from St. Cloud Normal, was on summer vacation from her teaching post at a school in Albert Lea, Minnesota. That summer gave rise to a solid relationship between Omar and Mary, and, after Bradley returned to West Point in the fall, the pair exchanged letters every week, never missing a one.

Bradley's third ("cow") and fourth West Point years were entirely engulfed by sports. As a yearling, he at last won a coveted position on the varsity football team, as a substitute center, earning a football letter even as he earned two letters in baseball, and his final year brought promotion to first sergeant of F Company, followed by promotion to cadet lieutenant. But, during the last half of Bradley's West Point career, athletics overshadowed both the eruption of World War I in Europe, beginning at the end of July 1914, and his own dedication to academics. Indeed, the "European war" made virtually no impact on either the life or curriculum of West Point. No one studied it. No one reported on it. No one even spoke much about it. For the Class of 1915, the battles of the American Civil War, long past, provided virtually all of the practical lessons presented on strategy and tactics—never mind that Grant and Lee had had no machine guns, 88-milimeter artillery, poison gas, airplanes, tanks, or other motorized vehicles. As for Bradley's academic performance, his class standing of 49 slipped to 53 at the end of his second year. He pulled this up to 43 in his third year, but, in June 1915, graduated 44th out of a class that had been winnowed down to 164. In later life, Bradley admitted that, had he concentrated less on sports and more on academics, he most likely could have graduated about 20th in his class. Yet he never regretted his sports obsession for a moment, due to its relevance to the life of a soldier:

> It is almost trite to observe that in organized team sports, one learns the important art of group cooperation in goal achievement. No extracurricular endeavor I know of could better prepare a soldier for the battlefield. West Point sports also gave me an excellent opportunity to take the measure of many men who would serve with, or under, me in World War II. It is noteworthy, I think, that all the men on our 1914 baseball team who remained in the army went on to become generals.[6]

The close equation of team athletic competition and the military art was hardly peculiar to Bradley. Eisenhower, Patton, Douglas MacArthur, and others felt the same way. It is not that Bradley and the rest thought of war as a game, but that they took athletics as seriously as they did war. Both were instances of the agon, a conflict pitting strategist against strategist and tactician against tactician, but, most of all, will against will, as well as testing the physical prowess and endurance of each adversary—not to mention their luck. Given the narrow engineering focus of the West Point curriculum at the time and the tactical and strategic concentration on antiquated battles, it is quite possible that team sport, so revered at the academy, was actually the most valuable military preparation the institution offered.

┼═══┤├

West Point was small in 1915, and so was the class of brand-new second lieutenants graduated that year—even though it was then the largest class to date. The army these young men would lead was likewise small: just 100 thousand men under the command of 5 thousand officers. When he had graduated in 1909, Patton wrestled anxiously with the question of what branch to choose. He opted finally for the cavalry, because he felt that it offered the greatest opportunity for front-line combat. When he graduated in 1915, Bradley found no reason to struggle over the choice. He did not concern himself with his position on the battlefield, but focused instead on the fact that, small as the army was, it was not easy to make a life's career in this service. The pace of promotion in the peacetime army was glacial, so Bradley, like most other West Point graduates at the time, sought a commission in one of the two branches in which promotion was the least slow—the engineers and field artillery. Cadets were expected to list three choices, in order of preference, and Bradley applied for engineers, artillery, and infantry, in that order. His class standing was not high enough to get him into his first two choices (though, at 44, he had outperformed Eisenhower, who stood at 61), so he settled for infantry. (That his lazy, slow-witted, and habitually disobedient roommate, Bennie Mills, graduating five places from the bottom, chose the aviation section of the Signal Corps speaks volumes for how the army of 1915 rated the future of military aviation.)

Any disappointment Bradley felt at failing to enter the engineers or the artillery faded when, within a year of his graduation, the army officially ended the practice of "branch promotion," so that all officers in every branch were placed on an equal footing—which meant a footing equally slow in promotion. Moreover, Bradley soon came to the realization that infantry, traditionally celebrated as the "queen of battle," was the branch in which, "more than any other . . . a soldier learns the art of leadership and command and, ultimately, has the best chances of reaching the topmost positions."[7] Not by any reason of prudence, wisdom, or perspicacity, Bradley's third choice turned out to be the best of all. It was, once again, the lesson of the playing field. Personal character, strategic and tactical skill, teamwork, strength, endurance, and courage were all important to victory, but good luck was indispensable.

CHAPTER 3

Left Out

Two photographs of "Omar Nelson Bradley, Moberly, Missouri" appeared on page 55 of the 1915 *Howitzer,* the West Point yearbook, and in both he was in uniform—one depicted him in the frogged and choke-collared trappings of a cadet, the other in the jersey of a baseball player. Like many other college yearbooks, the *Howitzer* sought to nail the character of the new graduate and predict his future. Unlike some, it made a remarkably accurate job of it.

Ike Eisenhower wrote the description of Bradley in the *Howitzer.* It began: "A buck for three years, he decided that during his first class year he'd wear a few chevrons himself, and after drilling the plebes in rudiments for three weeks came over to camp as 'F' Co. top."[1] In civilian English, Eisenhower meant that, after three years as a private, Bradley was catapulted to sergeant in his senior year and held that rank for just three weeks before being promoted to first (top) sergeant of F Company. By graduation, he was a cadet lieutenant. It was a progress predictive of the rest of his career. He would benefit from a burst in promotions during World War I, then advance at a glacial pace until America's entry into World War II, during which his rise would be meteoric.

What his classmate wrote about Bradley's character was even more incisive. He continued: "His greatest passion is baseball; football and 'F' Co. come next in order of rank," an observation only half in jest. "Many an opposing player has trifled once with Brad's throwing arm," Ike observed, "but never twice. And a batting average of .383 is never to be sneezed at." More importantly, the brief narrative addressed Bradley's loyalty and identification with his men: "[Y]ou couldn't pry him loose from 'F' Co. with a jimmy or a percy. He swears at, by, and for the Second Battalion Flankers, and witness his now famous remark—'Sir, I would rather be first sergeant of "F" Co. than captain of any other company.' And he really meant it." Ike called "getting there" Bradley's "most prominent characteristic"—not brilliance or audacity, but endurance and determination. All graduates profiled in the *Howitzer* were associated with an apposite quotation. For Bradley, Eisenhower chose "True merit is like a river, the deeper it is, the less noise it makes," and he closed his portrait with, "some day [we will] be bragging to our grandchildren that 'sure, General Bradley was a classmate of mine.'"[2]

Bradley's class graduated into a world at war, but one in which the United States was not yet involved. Instead, there was a brushfire conflict under way, a border skirmish with revolution-racked, revolution-weary Mexico that would soon explode into the so-called Punitive Expedition, against Pancho Villa. First Lieutenant George S. Patton Jr. and other like-minded officers on the make were eager to get involved in the shooting with Mexico, but Bradley, like most of his fellow graduates, had no desire to serve on the dusty and disagreeable Mexican border. Classmate Ike Eisenhower opted for the Philippines, but ended up on border duty just the same. Bradley chose service with the 14th Infantry, an outfit based in the Pacific Northwest. In contrast to Patton, who longed for action at every opportunity, Bradley "preferred to begin [his] career in a 'normal garrison' atmosphere."[3]

Granted three months' "graduation leave", Bradley returned to Moberly for the summer and spent much of his time playing right field for the semi-pro Moberly Athletes. He also saw a lot of Mary Quayle, now a rising senior at the University of Missouri, and found himself increasingly attracted to this young woman who was as much unlike himself as she was like his mother. "Endlessly fascinating," Bradley wrote later in life, "pretty, bright, ambitious and domineering."[4] Before the summer ended, Bradley gave Mary a white gold ring with a small solitaire diamond. Now officially engaged, they set a wedding date in June 1916, immediately after Mary's graduation.

In the meantime, Omar Bradley became acquainted with the army of a United States so committed to isolationism that it had trouble even imagining itself ever having to go to war. He reported to the 14th Infantry on September 12, 1915. Under the command of Colonel R. H. Wilson, it consisted of three battalions, all significantly understrength—as was virtually every unit of the diminutive peacetime force. The bare resources of the 14th were broadcast widely over the Northwest: 1st Battalion was posted in Alaska, 2nd stationed near Seattle, Washington, and the 3rd, to which Bradley was assigned, was quartered at Fort George Wright, outside of Spokane in the Rocky Mountains' western foothills. The battalion commander was Captain A. J. Harris; that the army did not elevate the commander of a battalion to major was not a reflection on Harris, but spoke volumes about an army reluctant to pony up a major's salary for a job it believed a captain could do. Wilbur A. McDaniel, Bradley's company commander, was also a captain, the rank appropriate to a company commander. Bradley noted that he was a good soldier, but, having been commissioned 17 years earlier, during the Spanish-American War, had yet to rise above the level of company captain. K Company's first sergeant, Ernest M. Johnson, was another longtime veteran—a man of so much experience that, while he was a noncommissioned officer (noncom) in the Regular Army, he simultaneously held the rank of major in the reserves. It was typical of Second Lieutenant Bradley that he respected and valued his commanding officer equally with the company's top noncom. From First Sergeant Johnson, he said, he learned much, including how to type. That meant a lot to him; for Bradley was an officer who valued concrete, specific, practical skills every bit as much as he admired theoretical knowledge, a facility with tactics, or a genius for strategy.

As for the privates of K Company—the typical understrength army company, mustering 60 or 70 men instead of the customary 100—they were, most of them, long-timers, paid, even after years of service, the private's salary of $13 a month and unable to look forward to the modest addition of a corporal's second stripe for even more years. "Why any of them joined the Army almost defies explanation," Bradley marveled.[5] It was a revelatory musing, suggesting Bradley's deep and basic respect for the ordinary soldier even as it betrayed the fact that, for Bradley, the army had never been an irresistible calling.

Working among gray-haired captains, veteran sergeants, and aging privates in a little fort at the end of the Spokane trolley line, young Bradley must have frequently doubted his future. On the other hand, the life he had with two other second lieutenants sharing a three-bedroom duplex, served by a paid black cook (who prepared meals for the three roommates and two other bachelor officers), was an easy and inexpensive existence, well within a second lieutenant's monthly salary of $141.67.

And then there was also the invaluable tutelage of the man who occupied the other half of the duplex. Edwin Forrest Harding, a graduate of the West Point class of 1909, was 29 years old, a six-year infantry veteran and still a second lieutenant. He was "a serious student of history, a fine writer and a compulsive teacher." The son of a schoolteacher, Bradley always gravitated to strong pedagogues, whether it was his company commander—himself a former schoolteacher—or Harding, a teacher by natural inclination. When Forest organized informal weekly gatherings, inviting a half-dozen lieutenants to his home for discussion of small-unit tactics and also military history, Bradley eagerly attended. Harding began Bradley's conversion from a young man who had taken a job with the military after getting an education on the army's dime into a real U.S. Army officer, instilling "a genuine desire to thoroughly learn my profession."[6]

The "profession" of a garrison officer in 1915 was, above all, relaxed. The workday morning, which began about seven o'clock, was devoted to four hours of drilling the men, which included some shooting, occasional platoon- or squad-level attack simulations, and a great deal of marching. When this was concluded, at 11:00 A.M., there was "officers' call," to which all officers were summoned to discuss issues and problems relating to the post and to receive the latest regulations and general orders. This was followed by lunch, after which the day was entirely free. Bradley wiled away his afternoons hiking or going to the movies in Spokane. In the fall of 1915, he bought a Winchester pump-action shotgun and, in company with Sergeant Johnson, hunted grouse.

The onset of winter was sufficiently bitter to incite a number of men to deliberately break army regulations by going AWOL in the expectation of being arrested and getting hot food and warm lodging in the guardhouse. For these dead-end soldiers, a cozy cell was infinitely preferable to cold duty out of doors. The flaw in the philosophy of these miscreants was their failure to think beyond the warmth of the guardhouse, which was, after all, no more than a holding pen for a court-martial to come, a proceeding that could result in dishonorable discharge and possibly even significant jail time. The tiny pre–World War I army habitually made do with what it had, and that meant putting a captain in a major's job and fashioning ad hoc lawyers out of officers who had never seen the inside of a courtroom. Such improvisation was especially the case at "frontier" outposts, and Bradley suddenly found himself detailed to defend the first man to come to trial. By way of preparation, he reviewed the smattering of law doled out to West Point cadets. His client was accused of being absent without leave and of stealing a suitcase. Bradley was able to create a reasonable doubt as to the identity of the thief and thereby obtained acquittal on the more serious grand larceny charge. This acquittal earned him an instant reputation, and all 33 remaining AWOLs put in requests for Second Lieutenant Bradley to serve as their defense counsel. He soon found himself relieved of the attorney's role, however, when he was appointed a member of the court and assigned to sit in judgment.

The earnest vigor with which Bradley threw himself into defending his soldier clients is early evidence of his sympathetic regard for the welfare of his men, and his superiors' choice of a shavetail second lieutenant to sit on the board of a court martial suggests the high regard in which senior command soon came to hold him. Another evidence of that esteem was Bradley's assignment to coach the boxers, wrestlers, high jumpers, and basketball players of Company K in the athletic competitions that were all-important in the peacetime army. Leading a company team to a winning season redounded to the credit of the company commander, who in turn valued the lieutenant who coached the team. Moreover, results of competitions routinely became part of official army records and made a difference when the coaching officer was up for promotion. That was important to Bradley, but so was keeping in top physical condition and getting to know his men—two more benefits of coaching.

<hr>

Looming over the adolescent idyll that was the peacetime U.S. Army of 1915 was the specter of war—not the "Great War" that was devastating Europe, but the prospect of war with Mexico, whose civil insurrection continually threatened to spill across the border. On January 10, 1916, Pancho Villa and his men attacked a train near Chihuahua, Mexico, executing 17 (some sources say 16) American citizens. Three months after this outrage, on March 9, 1916, he and his revolutionary División del Norte crossed the border to raid Columbus, New Mexico, killing 10 residents and 14 American soldiers, and wounding many others. President Woodrow Wilson responded by sending Brigadier General John J. Pershing on a "Punitive Expedition" to capture or kill Villa and his men. The year-long mission penetrated deeply into Mexico, and before it came to an end, Pershing was leading approximately 15 thousand troops while more than 150 thousand additional soldiers guarded the border. It was a mammoth operation for the tiny American army, and Bradley, like most other Americans, was certain that all-out war was imminent.

On May 9, the War Department called up National Guard units in Texas, New Mexico, and Arizona. At the same time, most units of the Regular Army, including Bradley's 14th Regiment, were ordered to the border. At 12:45 on the morning of May 11, Bradley boarded a troop train. Unlike Patton, who moved heaven and earth to secure himself a place on Pershing's staff in what he hoped would become a major shooting war, Bradley was torn by the necessity of postponing marriage to Mary Quayle in a ceremony planned for early June.

Steeling himself to the task, Bradley broke the news to Mary and left with his unit for Douglas, Arizona. There the 3rd Battalion of the 14th Regiment was joined by the 2nd (the 1st remained in Alaska) and by units of the Arizona National Guard. The entire assemblage pitched its tents in the desert east of town, adjacent to the camps of the 11th and 18th Infantry Regiments. Here were thousands of men, the greatest military presence Bradley had ever seen.

Girding for all-out war with the nation's southern neighbor sharply and suddenly nudged Washington out of its isolationist mood in a way that the distant "European war" could not. The National Defense Act of June 3, 1916 authorized a near doubling of the U.S. Army to 175 thousand men and transferred the National Guard largely out of state control and into federal authority. President Wilson used the new law to call up all 130 thousand National Guardsmen, sending most to the border. Omar Bradley could no longer think of himself as a second lieutenant in a company of 60 or 70 men. He was now part of a border force of 159 thousand—48 thousand Regulars (like himself) and 111 thousand Guardsmen—the greatest number of Americans under arms since the Spanish-American War.

Ongoing diplomatic discussions staved off and finally altogether avoided a major war, but, in the meantime, Bradley was tied down to the Douglas encampment, living in grim and tedious circumstances. He relieved the misery for himself and his troops by running a target range and coaching a 14th Regiment baseball team, and while Patton had made the army's first motorized assault—using three army automobiles to chase down one of Pancho Villa's top generals—Bradley participated in what he called "an epic experimental 200-mile 'motorized hike' with a convoy of trucks." To be sure, it was far less glamorous than Patton's dashing exploit—and it certainly did not make the papers—but it was at least equally important in the early development of the army's mechanization. Mechanized assault, of which both Patton and Bradley became staunch advocates, would play a key role in World War II tactics and strategy, but just as vital, and perhaps even more critical, was mechanized logistics. After the "experimental" convoy of 1916, the army would conduct many more "motorized hikes," including the spectacular 3,251-mile transcontinental convoy of July-September 1919, from Washington, D.C., to San Francisco, in which Bradley's classmate, Ike Eisenhower, took part. Their experience with such motorized hikes thoroughly persuaded both Bradley and Eisenhower of the paramount importance of logistics and acquainted them with both the potential and the limitations of vehicles in carrying out the logistical mission. As a mature commander in World War II, Bradley, for one, was convinced that the audacious and aggressive Patton, pioneer of the mechanized assault, never learned to fully appreciate the role of logistics in combat operations.[7]

On September 20, 1916, the 14th Regiment moved from Douglas to Yuma, Arizona. Although Bradley found Yuma "a no less disagreeable outpost" than Douglas, he gratefully reaped a major benefit from the war scare. Because the National Defense Act of 1916 had nearly doubled the size of the army, he and his classmates were automatically promoted from second to first lieutenant—after a mere 17 months' service. With this came a pay hike to $206 a month, which stood Bradley in good stead as he and Mary set a new wedding date of December 28, 1916.

By the end of the year, the danger of war with Mexico had passed, and Bradley was readily granted a month's leave, from December 7 to January 7. He reunited with Mary in Kansas City, after a 15-month absence, and the two were married, on the 28th, in the university town of Columbia, at the home of two good friends, Professor and Mrs. F. P. Spalding. Following a brief Kansas City honeymoon in a suite at the Muehlebach Hotel, the newlyweds worked their way westward by Pullman sleeping car. They stopped in El Paso to visit a West Point classmate, Jo Hunt "Spec" Reaney, who was serving with an infantry unit there. Bradley had arranged for a room in the elegant old Pasa del Norte Hotel, but perhaps more than for romance, the visit was to be a way of easing Mary into army life. He took her with him to lunch with Spec in a genuine U.S. Army mess tent, then, equally important by way of introduction to the army, Bradley, Spec, and Mary spent the afternoon watching an inter-company football game.

From El Paso, the couple continued by rail all the way to Los Angeles to visit two of Mary's aunts, stopping en route in Yuma so that Bradley could pick up his recently augmented pay. After spending time in L.A., the newlyweds returned to Yuma, on January 17, where they rented a small hilltop house—just two rooms and a screened porch, the kitchen and bedroom occupying the porch. That Bradley found duty in Yuma miserable suggests that it was even more trying for his bride. It is a measure of just how dull this life was that, a few weeks after settling in at Yuma, Bradley applied for transfer to 1st Battalion, posted at Tanana,

Alaska, in the remote wilderness, some five or six hundred miles up the Yukon River. When word came that the transfer had been approved, he and Mary were thrilled. Any place was better than Yuma.

But they would never get to Alaska.

President Woodrow Wilson had squeaked by to a second term as president of the United States in 1916 largely on the strength of his campaign slogan: "He kept us out of war." Nevertheless, the combined weight of Germany's resumption of unrestricted submarine warfare, of threats to the rights of the United States to navigate the high seas safely, of the infamous Zimmermann Telegram (by which Germany proposed to Mexico an alliance against the United States), of the increasingly hawkish sentiment of American business and banking interests (heavily invested in the Allies), and of Wilson's own visionary ambition to fight a war "to end all wars" and "make the world safe for democracy" pushed the president toward a declaration of war, which Congress approved on April 6, 1917. Thus the United States entered the European war, and the following month Congress passed a massive mobilization that would ultimately expand the Regular Army from its present actual strength of little over 100 thousand men to about 3.6 million by November 1918. On May 20, Bradley's battalion was ordered back to the Pacific Northwest, to Vancouver Barracks, Washington, and his orders to Alaska were summarily canceled.

Whether it was Alaska or Washington, both the Bradleys were overjoyed to leave Yuma, but, as "a professional soldier and a West Pointer," Bradley wanted more. He wanted desperately to "prove [his] mettle in a real war."[8]

Yet he entertained little hope of this happening: not as long as he was with the 14th Infantry. The scuttlebutt had it that the regiment's 1st Battalion was to remain indefinitely in Alaska, and there was no way that the War Department would send a regiment overseas absent one of its battalions. Bradley was convinced that the 14th was "doomed to a fate worse than death ... processing an endless stream of recruits," and unless he could transfer out of the regiment into one bound for France, he believed his career would be over before it began. For the next 16 months, he tried everything he could think of to get a transfer, but to no avail, and he sat out the "Great War" in utter frustration.[9]

Bradley had been wrong about one thing. The 14th did not spend the war processing recruits. Instead, in January 1918, the War Department assigned both the 2nd and 3rd Battalions to police the copper mines (and some other installations) in Montana. Copper was a strategically vital metal, and the Montana mines, long hotbeds of radical International Workers of the World (IWW) labor unrest, were perceived as vulnerable to violent work stoppages or even outright sabotage, which could seriously threaten the war effort. The duty fell far short of shipping out to France, but it gave First Lieutenant Bradley his first command, the five officers and eighty-six men of Company F, assigned to Butte.

If Yuma had been hot and desolate, Butte would prove frigid and lawless. Bradley ventured out in advance of his company to secure barracks facilities for his men and quarters for his officers. Arriving on January 26, he discovered that the mercury was frozen solid at 40 below zero and that everyone packed a gun as they strode the ugly streets of the ugly town. Into this rugged environment came Mary, seven and a half months pregnant, accompanied by her mother, Dora, who wanted to be available to help with the baby. The grim situation of Butte in winter grew instantly grimmer when, shortly after arriving in town, Mary went into labor and delivered a boy, stillborn. Dora Quayle boarded a train and escorted the infant's body back to Moberly, for burial in the Quayle family plot.

As for Bradley, he had little time to mourn. As had been feared, the IWW prepared to mount a St. Patrick's Day demonstration clearly intended to explode into an outright riot aimed at shutting down the Anaconda copper mines. Bradley had been tipped off to the plan and deployed his entire company throughout the town, whose Main Street teemed with thousands of angry men, many armed with knives and brass knuckles. F Company was understrength, but the sight of even 86 uniformed, helmeted men bearing loaded, bayonet-tipped rifles was sufficient to dissuade and deflate the would-be rioters.

+=≫≪=+

The pressures of a world war produced an avalanche of temporary promotions throughout the army's officer corps, and First Lieutenant

Bradley learned on August 14, 1918, that he had been jumped to temporary major. Although it was not an extraordinary step up in a time of national military emergency, it was evidence of the confidence Bradley's commanders had in him.

The promotion, temporary though it was, lifted Bradley's spirits. They positively soared the following month when he and the other men of the 14th Regiment learned that they were being ordered to Camp Dodge, near Des Moines, Iowa—and not only were the 2nd and 3rd Battalions to assemble there, but the 1st as well, urgently summoned from Alaska. This could mean only one thing. Bradley and the others were going to war.

⊢══⊣

Major Bradley was appointed to command 2nd Battalion, and the regiment reported to Camp Dodge on September 25, 1918, merging into the 19th Division there. Veteran officers, returned from France, were distributed throughout the division to subject these stateside troops to intensive field training in preparation for deployment. Bradley's professional horizon suddenly expanded and brightened.

But, yet again, outside forces intervened to shape the young officer's career path. By 1918, a disease the world called Spanish influenza—although it almost certainly originated in the United States, probably at Camp Funston, Kansas—had escalated beyond epidemic proportions and was becoming a global pandemic. The flu arrived at Camp Dodge shortly after the 14th Regiment, and men who had been spared death in the trenches of France began to fall in the plains of the American Midwest. Although the death rate overall was high, most victims of flu recovered, especially those, such as soldiers, who were young and fit. Nevertheless, the effects of the disease were debilitating, and convalescence was long. Camp Dodge, already jammed with new arrivals, was soon overwhelmed by sick men, its hospital filled to overflowing. Training was curtailed or suspended altogether, and, while many languished, rumors of peace drifted into camp. All of the European combatants were exhausted, bled white, but Germany had long been in the grip of an increasingly effective British naval blockade. The

German people were beginning to starve, and Kaiser Wilhelm II or his lieutenants started sending out tentative peace feelers.

That might be welcome news for the war-weary world, but Omar Bradley was just selfish enough to fear the effect peace would have on his career if he didn't get into the fight before it ended. Throughout October, the rumors of peace intensified in volume. From time to time, there was even word of an armistice. Each time, the news proved untrue, but by November there could be no doubt that peace was just around the corner. On the 11th of that month, Major and Mrs. Bradley were walking down a street in central Des Moines. Suddenly, the town's many factory whistles began to shrill. People surged out shop and office doorways and into the streets. There were shrieks, whoops, and an abundance of grateful tears. The Great War had ended at 11 A.M. Greenwich Mean Time (GMT), and word of the armistice had just reached this city in the heart of Iowa.

Did the Bradleys join the celebratory throng?

"I was glad the carnage had stopped," Bradley recalled many years later, "but I was now absolutely convinced that, having missed the war, I was professionally ruined." The landscape of Omar Nelson Bradley's life seemed now to stretch before him like the fields of Iowa in autumn, flat, gray, "a career lifetime of dull routine assignments," so that, after 30 years, he "would be lucky to retire . . . as a lieutenant colonel."[10]

CHAPTER 4

Shoestring Army

Omar Nelson Bradley saw no combat in the "Great War," but he was nevertheless part of an army that had burgeoned from something more than 100 thousand men in 1916 to 3.6 million by November 11, 1918. If that explosion was rapid, the implosion that followed the armistice was even faster. America went "demob mad," almost instantly shrinking the postwar army back to its puny prewar strength. Throughout most of the 1920s, the average strength of the Regular Army was 137,300 officers and men. By law, the National Guard was authorized at 435 thousand men, but a Congress eager to consummate what Woodrow Wilson's successor, Warren G. Harding, called a "return to normalcy," repeatedly whittled away at funding, allowing the Guard to maintain no more than about half its authorized numbers throughout the decade.

Bradley had joined a shoestring army and was accustomed to serving in one. What he was not prepared for was soldiering in a time of reactionary pacifism. The horror and waste of the Great War had not only made most Americans hate war, but also resent the military—and anything that smacked of militarism. It was not a good time to be a professional soldier, and the postwar army became increasingly insular and isolated from mainstream America. The 19th Infantry Division was among the first units to muster out, and Bradley soon found himself huddling with what remained of it, his own much-reduced 14th Regiment. He was assigned to move with this unit on December 11, 1918, from Camp Dodge, Iowa, to Camp Grant, Illinois, where he was to assist in the orderly closing of that facility and the salvage of government property there. He and Mary drove from Des Moines to Camp Grant, near Rockford, in a new Dodge sedan, for which the couple had shelled out $1,067.

They found Camp Grant a chaos of men in the process of demobilization. Worst of all, even as his battalion of the 14th Regiment worked feverishly to process out men and equipment, it, too, underwent demobilization, dwindling by the day, until Bradley had nothing left to command but a skeleton. When he found it impossible to scrape together even two or three squads, Bradley gave up on the idea of maintaining the customary routines of training and close-order drill. Living in a rented house off-base in Rockford, he passed much of the dreary Midwestern winter reading and talking endlessly with Mary about what duty he should next apply for. At length, the couple decided that they wanted to return to the Pacific Northwest—a region they had grown to love—and Bradley believed that the most rewarding career he could find in the badly atrophied postwar army was as a Reserve Officer Training Corps (ROTC) instructor in a college located somewhere in that region.

But the army had very different plans. On July 11, 1919, without prior notice or warning, Bradley was ordered to take charge of a thousand-man unit bound from San Francisco to Vladivostok, Russia, for duty in Siberia.

Siberia! To the stunned Bradley, it must have seemed a grotesque joke. Just when it would seem that army life could not possibly have become any more depressing for a young career officer, the army had found a way to make it so.

Yet again, however, chance intervened to spare Bradley. Back in March, he had been appointed to a court-martial board hearing the case of 16 African American soldiers who had been indicted for the gang-rape of a white woman. The complex and politically charged case was still dragging on in July when Bradley received his Siberian orders. The War Department had specifically barred the transfer of any member of the court until the case had been concluded; Bradley therefore telegraphed the War Department, which, to his infinite relief, revoked the Siberian transfer, leaving him free to follow through on his application for an ROTC instructorship.

In the army, assignment request forms are informally called "dream sheets," and the closest Bradley could come to realizing anything like a dream for himself and Mary was to find a billet in the Pacific Northwest. Accordingly, he carefully typed "Northwest" in the portion of the form asking for the applicant's desired location. It is a measure of Bradley's lingering heartland parochialism that he assumed "Northwest" meant Washington and Oregon. As far as the army was concerned, however, those states were part of the *Pacific* Northwest. Without that crucial modifier, "Northwest" designated North and South Dakota. On August 25, 1919, therefore, Bradley was assigned as assistant professor of military science and tactics at South Dakota State College of Agriculture and Mechanic Arts, in the tiny prairie town of Brookings.

It was hardly the dream prospect of life in the Cascades, but it was a lot better than Siberia, and the schoolteacher's son took to his assignment with enthusiasm. In the summer, he led an ROTC encampment in Michigan, followed by a three-week leave spent fishing in the lakes of Minnesota. Come August 1920, as he prepared for another academic year at Brookings, Bradley learned that although the shrinking army reduced opportunities for many (in 1921, budget cuts would force a thousand fully qualified officers into early retirement), it broadened his own horizon. At the close of August, he received a War Department telegram ordering him to West Point as an instructor in mathematics.

+≻═≺+

Assignment to West Point would have been an honor at any time, but Bradley found himself there during a period of particular challenge and opportunity. The demands of war had stripped the Corps of Cadets, so that 1919 was a year virtually without an organized body of students, and

1920, when Bradley reported, was a year of intense struggle toward some semblance of order. The prevailing chaos prompted Army Chief of Staff Peyton March to appoint Douglas MacArthur, son of the popular Medal of Honor winner Arthur MacArthur and a military hero in his own right, as superintendent of the academy. Bold, flamboyant, and unorthodox, MacArthur was expected to shake up the institution, to modernize it, and then to put it back into good order. He did just that, amid much controversy, making all manner of competitive intramural sport compulsory, banning all hazing, introducing a more mature, relaxed approach to discipline, and setting forth an ambitious plan to expand the Corps of Cadets from 13 hundred to almost 3 thousand—a program the parsimonious Congress never let get off the ground.

If the new superintendent was unconventional, so were the postwar cadets. The Class of 1924 was 400 strong—vast, by academy standards—and consisted of many men who were veterans of the fighting in France. In contrast to the mood prevailing throughout much of the rest of the army, West Point was in high morale and offered a rich social life—in which the staid Bradleys partook little. Overnight, Prohibition had transformed the United States into a nation of lawbreakers, and the quarters of West Point officers flowed freely with bootlegged whiskey, bathtub gin, and home-brewed beer, but neither Mary nor Omar Bradley drank—though Omar would soon learn to—nor, for that matter, smoked. Mary in particular disapproved of drunkenness and the oppressive scent of cigarettes. Avoiding big parties, she joined the wives of other officers in playing bridge, while her husband learned to become a skilled poker player.

Poker was more than a diversion for Bradley. The go-go twenties were not an inexpensive time, and Bradley, after the war, had reverted from major to captain (with a commensurate cut in pay), was briefly re-promoted, then again reduced, only to be promoted to the Regular Army rank of major in 1924. He would remain at this rank for the next dozen years. At $300 to $350 per month, even a major's pay was hardly munificent, but both Bradley and Mary were by nature frugal, and poker proved a sufficient way to supplement a modest income. Bradley approached the game as something of a second job, hedging his bets by religiously folding unless he clearly saw a 70 percent chance of winning. He always claimed that this disciplined and conservative strategy made his winning predictable and steady. (The couple needed all the money they could get. Feeling settled at West Point, Omar and Mary Bradley worked at starting a family. Mary initially miscarried, but she soon became pregnant again and, on December 3, 1923, Elizabeth Bradley was born.)

Calculating and disciplined poker play was both a window into Bradley's tactical and strategic philosophy and rehearsal for its future implementation. George S. Patton Jr., a far bolder gambler when it came to tactics as well as strategy, led a life he believed guided largely by destiny. In contrast, Bradley's experience in the world up to this point had persuaded him that life—*his* life, certainly—was made up in large measure of chance occurrences and their consequences, whether it was a casual conversation with a Sunday school superintendent that put him on an unlikely road to West Point or court-martial duty that saved him from exile to Siberia. Chance was a big part of a life, of a career—and of war. Bradley neither embraced nor shunned the concept of chance; instead, he accepted it, and he resolved to manage it. This he did chiefly by taking a conservative but positive approach to all things uncertain, basing his actions as far as possible on calculation.

+>==>=+

Bradley was by no means a standout mathematician, but the officer who chose him, Colonel Charles P. Echols, Class of 1891 and a West Point mathematics professor since 1904, had been Bradley's own instructor. He saw in him an apt pupil, and whereas Bradley had finished his first, or "plebe," year a respectable 49th overall, he stood at number 32 in mathematics, which was very good indeed. He undertook his assignment with enthusiasm and great interest. The source of the enthusiasm he instinctively understood as something of a tribute to his father, and the source of his interest was the opportunity the assignment afforded for a "prolonged immersion in math," which Bradley understood as the study of logic. He would later write that his background in mathematics provided him with the logical decision-making skills needed when "faced with infinitely complex problems, often requiring immediate life-or-death decisions."[1]

Assigned to teach "plebe math"—freshman basic geometry and algebra—he nevertheless voluntarily attended math refresher classes five afternoons a week. Evenings he devoted to cramming for the very lesson he was expected to teach his plebes the next morning. As full as his days and evenings were, Bradley, like all junior officer-instructors at the academy during the MacArthur regime, was also expected to serve as a coach in one of the new intramural athletic programs. For Bradley, baseball would have been the obvious and ideal coaching assignment, but, in the best army tradition, he was tapped instead to coach soccer, about which he knew nothing. He eagerly accepted another officer's offer to swap football for soccer. The other man, Lehman W. Miller, had played neither soccer nor football, but, "since I knew football, he suggested we trade coaching jobs so that the company would receive expertise in at least one sport."[2] On the face of it, this was far from an ideal solution, but Bradley thought the logic inescapable nevertheless. He coached a championship intramural football team, and, as it turned out, Miller rose to the occasion as well. His soccer squad also finished the season as champions. The coaching solution exhibited what would prove to be Bradley's customary pragmatism. Rather than pine for an unattainable ideal, you do the best with what you have.

⊢══━⊣

Four years was the customary length of an assignment as a West Point instructor. By his final year at the academy, 1923–1924, Bradley had risen to the academic rank of associate professor of mathematics and was now teaching the afternoon refresher course he had taken as a new instructor. There loomed in this final year the question of where to go next. In contrast to more colorful commanders, such as MacArthur and Patton, Bradley always accepted the notion of working within the system. Convention prescribed that, after an unbroken succession of stateside duties, Bradley should apply for an assignment overseas. But the peacetime interwar army provided a narrow range of such posts, limited to Puerto Rico, Panama, Hawaii, and the Philippines. Of these, Bradley settled on Puerto Rico, but what he really wanted to do was to begin his advanced military education by enrolling in the Infantry School at Fort Benning, Georgia, vital and all but obligatory preparation for field command in that service branch. Longstanding military custom virtually dictated, however, that an officer not transfer from service at one school directly into an assignment at another. So Bradley prepared to move to Puerto Rico as a way station on his road to Benning. On the verge of finalizing his transfer request, he learned that his fellow West Point instructor Matthew Ridgway had successfully tapped a War Department connection that enabled him to break with custom and proceed directly from a West Point instructorship to Benning. With a new precedent thus established, Bradley followed suit, withdrawing his request for duty in Puerto Rico and asking for assignment to the Infantry School. He was accepted in the year-long senior officers' advanced course.

+━━◆━━+

Bradley left for Infantry School feeling that his four years at West Point had been of great benefit to him as a professional soldier, prompting him to begin what he saw as the serious study of military history and biography, a process of "learning a great deal from the mistakes of my predecessors." Of particular interest was William Tecumseh Sherman, who he believed was the ablest general the Union had produced. From his perspective as a young officer in the army of the 1920s, what especially struck Bradley about Sherman was his mastery of "the war of movement," whereas the leadership of the U.S. Army after the Great War was mostly fixated on static trench combat. Bradley had believed that his failure to get into the European war irreparably damaged his career, but now he glimpsed a positive advantage in not having personally experienced the trenches. He was not committed to static strategy and tactics, and he could freely imagine alternatives to them. Studying Sherman—"to the exclusion of World War I battle reports"—he came to the conclusion that the "rapid, sweeping mass movement of forces deep into the enemy's heartland was the best way to destroy an enemy army."[3] Bradley was on his way to becoming an advocate of blitzkrieg, or lightning war, well before the word for the tactic that defined both the opening and closing of World War II in Europe had even come into existence.

Primed by his study of General Sherman, Bradley found Infantry School at Fort Benning a revelation. It was, as army institutions go, a new school, just six years old, and, in contrast to most of the rest of the army, it was resolutely forward looking, emphasizing open warfare—Sherman's "war of maneuver." Bradley soon discovered that his classmates who had served in France found it difficult to adjust themselves to the concept, whereas he, who had seen no trench warfare, maintained an open mind, which eagerly took in the doctrine and technical details relating to troop movement and mechanization as well as the use of machine guns, mortars, automatic rifles, and the 37-mm gun, the infantry weapons that were the staple of modern war and about which Bradley had known nothing.

Of all the aspects of the curriculum at Benning, Bradley most enjoyed working outdoors with the demonstration troops of the 29th Infantry. Before he graduated from Infantry School, Bradley acquired a reputation as a specialist in tactics and terrain—"fire and movement"—which set him apart from many officers senior to him.

As ahead of the times as the Infantry School was in its emphasis on open warfare, Bradley later came to recognize that it nevertheless trailed the state of the military art as practiced by the most advanced European armies. Its most serious doctrinal shortcoming, Bradley ultimately concluded, was twofold: a failure to deal with the tank and the airplane, and a failure to envision the coordination of the tank and the airplane—armor and air—with infantry operations. Despite this, he took pride lifelong in graduating from the advanced course ranked number two in his class, below the brilliant Leonard T. "Gee" Gerow, an officer senior to him.

Top performance in Infantry School was a qualification for field command as well as a prerequisite for moving on to an even more prestigious school. Officers who had their eye on command at the highest levels enrolled first in the Command and General Staff School and then in the Army War College, the latter reserved for those men earmarked as general-officer material. The trailblazing example of Ridgway might have made it possible to advance directly from teaching at West Point to enrollment in the Infantry School, but moving seamlessly from Benning to Leavenworth—home of the Command and General Staff School—was out of the question. Bradley would have to take his long-delayed overseas duty, with troops, first. He no longer set his sights on Puerto Rico, however, but aimed higher, drawing a bead on one of the postwar army's most appealing billets: the U.S. Territory of Hawaii, then as now considered a Pacific paradise. He was thrilled when his request for duty there was approved.

After arriving in Honolulu on September 8, 1925, Major Bradley was briefly assigned to the 19th Infantry Regiment before being given command of 1st Battalion, 27th Infantry Regiment, 22nd Brigade. Both the brigade commander, Brigadier General Stewart Heintzelman, and the regimental commander, Colonel Laurence Halstead, had served in France during the war, yet Bradley was fortunate in that neither was the typical hidebound advocate of trench warfare. They wanted their men to receive the best and most modern tactical training possible, and they were eager to have a Fort Benning graduate who had absorbed the emerging doctrine of open warfare.

Heintzelman and Halstead provided a salubrious professional climate in which Major Bradley could train his men, even as he honed his own tactical skills. Hawaii itself furnished the natural climate and terrain Bradley found ideal for field training. Contrary to the popular mythology of World War II, which paints the 1941 attack on Pearl Harbor as a complete surprise, the American military was keenly aware of deteriorating relations between the United States and Japan and of what the likely consequences of that deterioration would be. Strategists in Washington developed Plan Orange, a blueprint for the defeat of Japan should that nation move against America in the Pacific. Hawaii was the most important base from which a counterattack against Japan would be staged, and the principal mission of the Hawaiian Division, of which Bradley was now a part, was to defend Pearl Harbor and ward off any attempt to invade Oahu. Bradley's tactical training and planning were therefore more than mere academic exercises. They were carried out with the division's mission in mind, and that mission gave an acute focus to all that Bradley did. He decided that his most important task was to lead tactical training in the field and on terrain.

There is a world of difference between plotting maneuvers on flat maps and executing them on the three dimensions of actual ground.

Bradley devoted much time and effort to building intricate and accurately scaled sand tables—essentially large-scale, horizontally placed relief maps—for the officers and noncommissioned officers to study and work with. The most notable of history's captains—Hannibal, Napoleon Bonaparte, General Robert E. Lee, and Bradley's favorite, Sherman—shared an uncanny feel for the ground, a thoroughgoing sense of what modern military planners call the battlespace. Bradley worked hard to develop such a sense in himself—and, ever the mentor, to impart it to those under his command and tutelage. Bradley's aim was to create realistic training, both in the field and in the planning rooms of headquarters. In this, he both anticipated and helped to lay the foundation for military planning and training of today, both of which attempt to narrow the gap between field exercises and actual combat and between battle planning and the real-world battlespace.

Even with a serious mission earnestly carried out, Bradley had ample time for recreation on the beautiful island. He became an avid golfer, attacking the game four to five afternoons every week until he had knocked his handicap down to four strokes. At the end of one set of 18 holes, the 33-year-old consumed his first glass of whiskey (of necessity bootlegged)—and liked it enough to make "a habit of having a bourbon and water or two (but never more) before dinner" for the rest of his life.[4]

Bradley also had time and opportunity to meet a fellow major, the G–2 (chief intelligence officer) of the Hawaiian Division, George S. Patton Jr., who lived across the street from the Bradleys' Schofield Barracks quarters. George and Beatrice Patton were a wealthy couple at the epicenter of the social life of Hawaii's military circle. The Bradleys were quiet, even retiring, and therefore saw little of the Pattons for some time. Besides, cavalryman Patton had no use for golf. Outdoors, he believed, a man's time was best spent on the back of a horse—and infantryman Bradley did not much like horses. But when Patton decided to recruit a competitive trapshooting team, he reached out to Bradley, having heard he was a good shot. Bradley accepted Patton's invitation to try out for the team. After missing the first two shots, he hit numbers three through twenty-three in a row. With neither a handshake nor a smile, Patton muttered, "You'll do." For his part, Bradley did not jump at the offer. Patton was already infamous throughout Oahu for his aggressive flamboyance, his impulsive temper and temperament, his hard drinking, his arrogance, and, not least of all, his compulsive need to shock any and all within earshot with outrageous or just plain vulgar pronouncements. "I was not certain I wanted to be on the team," Bradley recalled many years later. "Patton's style did not at all appeal to me." Ultimately, however, he "signed on for the sport of it."[5]

+≒≒+

Omar Bradley's Hawaiian idyll—20 months commanding 1st Battalion, 27th Infantry—came to an abrupt end on June 9, 1927, when he was appointed officer in charge of National Guard, Reserve, and ROTC affairs for the Hawaiian Department. The duty largely boiled down to serving as liaison between the Regular Army and the Hawaiian National Guard, setting training standards and overseeing all aspects of administration. It was desk work, neither very taxing nor very interesting.

The standard Hawaiian tour in the interwar army was three years, but many officers, in love with the country and the climate, requested and were granted extensions. The Bradleys likewise found Hawaii a delicious place, but Major Bradley believed he had been slotted into a dead end with the National Guard, and so he requested a return to the mainland. To his great satisfaction, he was ordered, on April 8, 1928, to Fort Leavenworth, Kansas, and the Command and General Staff School. Kansas was not Hawaii, to be sure, but the appointment was an honor and a professional vote of confidence. Ever mindful of his lack of combat experience, the modest Bradley did not quite see stars in his military future, but he believed that successful completion of the school course would at least guarantee him promotion to colonel by the time he retired.

After trading in the family Buick on a new Hudson (to be picked up on the mainland), the Bradleys boarded the U.S. Army transport *Cambria* on May 28, 1928, spent the summer in Moberly, then drove on to Leavenworth in September. The Command and General Staff School was second only to the War College in prestige, but Bradley soon came to believe that its reputation was built more on what high grades at the school would do for promotion than real academic and military excellence;

Bradley judged the problems and solutions presented in school lectures to be "trite, predictable and often unrealistic."[6]

A more daunting challenge than the unimaginative course work were the chronic oral abscesses and infections Bradley endured as the long-lingering result of the blow to the teeth he had suffered in his ice-skating accident at age 17. Told by a Fort Leavenworth physician that his recurrent dental problems could ultimately affect his heart, the bacteria infecting the heart valves, bringing on irreversible heart disease and even a heart attack, Bradley reluctantly followed the doctor's advice to have all of his teeth extracted.

Bradley performed well at the Command and General Staff School, and although he found many of the problems and much of the instruction disappointing, he believed that he had profited from his year at Leavenworth. At the very least, he was introduced to a higher level of war planning, a level of broad strategy, not applied to companies, battalions, regiments, or brigades, but to entire corps, armies, and theaters of war. Even the very predictability of so much that had been presented offered a valuable lesson, he thought: "When the 'conventional' solution to a complex military problem is already well known by rote, unconventional—and often better—solutions are more likely to occur."[7] That is, to be creative and innovative—to be truly unconventional—a commander must first be thoroughly grounded in the conventional, no matter how tried, true, and trite.

As usual, the end of one assignment brought the necessity of choosing the next. Bradley was offered a choice to return to West Point as treasurer of the academy or to return to Fort Benning, this time as an instructor at the Infantry School. Although Mary lobbied for the civilized comforts of the academy, Bradley preferred the informality of Fort Benning. More important, he believed that a tour as instructor there would be far more beneficial to his career than a stint as West Point treasurer. Bradley came to consider his choice to return to the Infantry School the most fortunate of his life.

CHAPTER 5

Foot Soldier in "Marshall's Revolution"

Like millions of other Americans, the Bradleys suffered serious financial loss in the stock market crash of October 1929. The family arrived at Fort Benning about $5,000 in the hole. In contrast to many others, however, Omar Nelson Bradley had a job and sound credit. He covered the family's losses with a loan, reluctantly obtained, and took comfort in his new assignment. The Infantry School at Fort Benning had undergone a major transformation since he had left it, as a new graduate, four years earlier. It no longer had the rough-and-ready look of a hastily established military facility, but had acquired the polish of a permanent post, with pleasant quarters and a new nine-hole golf course. More important, Bradley soon discovered, it had been utterly transformed in spirit and doctrine through the work of "one of the greatest military minds the world has ever produced: George Catlett Marshall."[1]

Omar Bradley was not a man given to idolatry, but he came close in two instances: with his own father, and with Marshall, "the most impressive man I ever knew."[2] Marshall was not a product of West Point, but of the Virginia Military Institute (VMI)—Class of 1901. He subsequently graduated first in his class from what was in 1907 the Infantry and Cavalry School at Fort Benning, passed through the Staff College there, then, as a first lieutenant, taught in the Leavenworth U.S. Army schools from 1908 to 1910. In World War I, he served as a staff officer with the 1st Division and then as division operations officer, helping to plan the first American attack in France. After promotion to temporary colonel in July 1918, he was assigned the following month to the headquarters of American Expeditionary Force (AEF) commander John J. Pershing, becoming chief architect of the ambitious American Saint-Mihiel Offensive (Sept. 12–16, 1918). This was a heady assignment, and achievement, for a young officer, and one of great consequence to AEF operations, but what doubtless impressed Bradley even more was Marshall's command role in the transfer of 500 thousand men and 2,700 guns from Saint-Mihiel to the culminating Allied offensive of the war at Meuse-Argonne. While not as "glorious" as the battles at Saint-Mihiel and Meuse-Argonne, this masterpiece of logistics and staff management was among the AEF's most significant achievements in the war. It earned Marshall appointment as chief of operations for the First U.S. Army in October 1918, followed by elevation to chief of staff of VIII Corps in November.

⊢⊷⊶⊣

In 1927, Marshall was appointed assistant commandant of the Infantry School, bringing to the job the résumé of a much older officer combined with the revolutionary spirit of a man who was still young in his forties. As assistant commandant, Marshall exercised almost total authority over designing the academic program of the Infantry School, and he fully understood the importance of his assignment and his authority. He was charged with creating and implementing a curriculum that would teach company-grade officers (lieutenants and captains) small-unit tactics and that would also train enlisted men to become trainers themselves, in the event of mobilization. Additionally, the Infantry School was to develop and test new infantry tactics and doctrine. Marshall in particular wanted to disseminate the ideas Pershing had developed during the war, especially the concept of combat built on firepower and maneuverability. This concept had most often been at odds with the static nature of trench warfare as practiced by the French and the British, and Pershing also found it difficult to implement during the war because American military officers—especially those of company grade—had never received any training to prepare them for "open warfare" or the "war of maneuver." Having witnessed Pershing's frustration, Marshall was determined to redress these inadequacies of doctrine and training. Like Bradley, he believed the future of combat was in offensive movement, not static defense. Throughout most of the "Great War," technology had favored the defenders: the trench was without question a defensive fortification, and the machine gun (weapon par excellence of that war) was chiefly a defensive weapon, allowing two or three men, firing from static cover, to kill hundreds of mobile attackers. By the end of the war, however, the technology of attack—of movement—was beginning to overtake that of defense. The airplane, the tank, and other motorized vehicles were rapidly coming into their own. Pershing had entered the war critical of the Allies' stubborn adherence to static trench tactics, which, he believed, had brought the struggle to a bloody stalemate. Marshall was certain that the next war would *begin* with attack and movement, and that whoever mastered these would emerge victorious.

To Omar Bradley, the assistant commandant appeared as a kindred spirit. He was thrilled as Marshall lectured, inviting both students and instructors to "Picture the opening campaign of a war":

> It is a cloud of uncertainties, haste, rapid movements, congestion on the roads, strange terrain, lack of ammunition and supplies at the right place at the right moment, failures of communications, terrific tests of endurance, and misunderstandings in direct proportion to the inexperience of the officers and the aggressive action of the enemy. Add to this a minimum of preliminary information of the enemy and of his dispositions, poor maps, and a speed of movement in alteration of the situation, resulting from fast flying planes, fast moving tanks, armored cars, and

motor transportation in general. There you have warfare of movement. . . . That, gentlemen, is what you are supposed to be preparing for.[3]

It was all a very far cry from the "trite" and "predictable" problems offered at the Command and General Staff School, and a thirsty Bradley greedily drank it in.

Omar Bradley was one of 80 Benning instructors in whom Marshall was determined to inculcate the gospel of open warfare, even in the face of "the technique and practices [previously] developed at Benning and Leavenworth [which] would practically halt the development of an open warfare situation, apparently requiring an armistice or some understanding with a complacent enemy."[4]

In addition to developing and disseminating new doctrine and new tactics, Marshall insisted on instituting eminently practical fire-and-maneuver exercises, which encouraged, and even demanded student initiative. In the past, instructors handed student lieutenants and captains long and detailed field orders, which they were expected to carry out to the letter and with a minimum of original thought. Under Marshall, students were presented not with instructions, but with problems, and then told to solve them.

The movement, speed, and confusion that Marshall believed would characterize the next war did not permit the luxury of complexity, especially since most of the army fighting that war would consist of conscripted citizen soldiers, not professional men at arms. Marshall exhorted his instructors: "Expunge the bunk." Fully embracing reality, he stressed rigorous simplification as an alternative. "We must develop a technique and methods so simple that the citizen officer of good common sense can readily grasp the idea."[5]

To those who were receptive, like Bradley, those who would learn, invent, and implement the new ideas, Marshall was a great mentor. To those in whom a like passion was not kindled, to Benning instructors who refused to adapt or who were incapable of adapting, Marshall simply showed the door. He made little effort to convert the conservative faculty of the Infantry School into innovators. Instead, he concentrated on training a generation of innovators—and he fired the conservatives. This was in itself one of the most valuable command lessons Bradley learned from George Marshall. Later in life, Bradley wrote that he had imbibed from Marshall the very "rudiments of effective command," and they consisted of this: "If a man performed, you left him alone. If not, you either bucked him up or sacked him." Marshall, Bradley saw, was never one to hover or micromanage. "After once having assigned an officer to his job General Marshall seldom intervened"—except to remove and replace him if he faltered or failed.[6]

Marshall had been leading the "Benning Revolution"—also called "Marshall's Revolution"—for two years by the time Bradley arrived to teach at the Infantry School. Marshall had assembled a four-man academic team to carry out his program of reform. Joseph Stilwell headed the tactical section of the curriculum; Lieutenant Colonel Morrison C. Stayer was in charge of the logistical section; Lieutenant Colonel Ralph W. Kingman had responsibility for weapons; and Bradley's good friend Forrest Harding relished control over military history and publications. As Bradley saw it, these men shared with Marshall a "keen analytic intelligence, outspokenness, [and] ingenuity. In sum, they were, like Marshall, highly creative."[7]

Although all Benning instructors, or at least all those who survived, came under Marshall's overall direction, Bradley's immediate superior during his first year as an Infantry School instructor was Stilwell. "Vinegar Joe," as the press would aptly dub him during World War II, was possessed of a personality even more challenging than Marshall's. Citing an essay Stilwell wrote to his family in which he described himself as "unreasonable, impatient, sour-balled, sullen, mad, hard, profane, vulgar," Bradley commented in his posthumously published autobiography: "I would not disagree with any of those adjectives." However, he continued, "I would hasten to add several others: professional, visionary, ingenious, aesthetic, athletic (at forty-six, he still ran several miles a day)." Bradley considered himself supremely fortunate to be assigned to teach tactics—specifically, battalion-level attack—under Stilwell. [8]

Both Marshall and Stilwell were so intent on replacing rote tradition with fresh invention that they banned instructors from using lecture notes. Classroom lectures were instead to be delivered extemporaneously.

Bradley was a natural teacher, but he was hardly a natural orator. For his first lecture, he improvised a pair of training wheels by drawing up a handful of note cards with subject headings in heavy black print. These he positioned at his feet, behind the lectern, so that he could glance down when he felt the need of a prompt. That, however, was the first and the last time he cheated. Bradley soon discovered that he knew his material so thoroughly he had no need of a crib.

Although classroom work occupied much of his time, Bradley most relished outdoor field exercises. For him, they were a valuable education. To be sure, he had gone through plenty of field exercises when he himself had been a student at Benning, but instead of conducting them by the outmoded rules of pre-Marshall Benning, he focused on close study of terrain and simplifying effective, often improvised approaches to it. In the process, he discovered what many teachers discover sooner or later: that you do not truly *learn* a subject until you have *taught* it.

Not that, under the Marshall-Stilwell regime, one ever really *taught*. Instead, instructors facilitated learning, eliciting from students the best original thinking of which they were capable. "Any student's solution of a problem that ran radically counter to the approved school solution," Marshall decreed, "and yet showed independent creative thinking, would be published to the class." Stilwell put less of a fine point on the matter. He declared himself open to any "screwball idea."[9]

If anything, the open intellectual atmosphere that Marshall and Stilwell strove to create, and in which Bradley reveled, was far more demanding than instruction by-the-book, even when the book was highly complex. Marshall and Stilwell heightened the reality of the exercises by purposely creating confusion, such as by throwing in unexpected problems. Their object was never to elicit the "correct" answer, but always to "encourage almost instantaneous clear, correct, improvised solutions." Subjected to this as a student, Matthew Ridgway later recalled that it created a "mental conditioning [that was] more important to a combat officer than any number of learned techniques."[10] The point was this: if the next war was to be a war of movement—movement and fire at great velocity—then the most valuable command commodities would be simplicity, improvisation, ingenuity, and speed, not a set of neat and tidy answers to cookie-cutter exam questions.

If George C. Marshall earned a reputation for ruthlessness with regard to personnel, if he did not think twice about firing a nonperformer, he also eventually acquired commensurate notice as an officer who consistently groomed select individuals for the highest levels of command, not as a reward for personal loyalty, but in recognition of competence, talent, and a high degree of likelihood that the individual in question would contribute to the effectiveness of the army. Thus, when Marshall selected Bradley at the end of his first year to replace Kingman as chief of the weapons section, Bradley deemed it a great honor. As one of Marshall's four lieutenants, he was now on a par with Stilwell, Stayer, and Harding. Yet this hardly gave Bradley a warm and fuzzy feeling. For one thing, while postwar pacifism had taken a toll on the army, it was now under assault by the Great Depression as well. It was all well and good to talk about modern war-fighting doctrine, tactics, and weapons, but it was a tough proposition to prepare and train in grossly undermanned units (by 1930, the Regular Army consisted of just 138 thousand officers and men) that had precious little in the way of tanks, vehicles, modern weapons, or even ammunition. Add to this the unrelenting demands of George C. Marshall, and the chief's job was daunting indeed.

Bradley's first big test came at the very opening of the school term during his second year—and it was a test of his own making. In the past, the heads of the tactics, logistics, and history sections each delivered a daylong briefing to all staff instructors on the functions of the sections and what each intended to achieve with the students in the school year. The weapons section chief was not expected to give such a briefing, however, because it was assumed that knowledge of weapons was ingrained in all army officers. Moreover, Benning's firing ranges were not easily accessible by large numbers and did not lend themselves to demonstration. Catching the spirit of revolution, Bradley defied tradition by telling Marshall that, with recent developments in weapons technology, and the doctrine to go along with them, he had much to convey. He therefore asked for four hours one morning for a comprehensive outdoor show. Marshall agreed.

Bradley deemed his decision to stick his neck out with this demonstration one of the "most important of my peacetime career."[11] He also took great pride in the planning and execution of a highly complex demonstration consisting of no fewer than fourteen events in four hours. Clockwork precision would be required, since each event could be allotted a mere ten minutes, including travel time—the busing of the staff from one range to another. As Bradley saw it, there would not be enough time to allow each expert to deliver a briefing about his weapons system, so he himself would introduce the expert, deliver the briefing, then invite the officers to direct any questions to the expert. It was a genuine military operation, and Bradley approached it as such.

Bradley led his section staff—13 officers and several dozen enlisted men—together with all instructors and Marshall to the events. The entire demonstration was a marvel of efficiency, completed not in four hours, but in just two and a half. Marshall pronounced it the best demonstration he ever saw and asked Bradley to give it to every Infantry School class.

In this way, Omar Bradley approached the orbit of George C. Marshall. He actually entered that orbit when he befriended an outstanding student in the advanced class at the Infantry School, Captain Walter Bedell "Beetle" Smith, a veteran of combat in France who was destined to become Ike Eisenhower's right-hand man—his chief of staff—in World War II. At Benning, Bradley was impressed by Smith's analytical brilliance—and also his way with a rifle. Although Smith enrolled in one of his advanced classes, Bradley first got to know him when the young captain came to shoot on the trapshooting range Bradley had organized. The more time Bradley spent with the innately standoffish Smith ("brittle, like Stilwell, a bit of a Prussian, and brutally frank"), the more strongly he felt that he would make a superb instructor at the Infantry School. One day, Marshall visited Bradley's classroom while Smith was presenting a monograph on a subject Bradley had assigned. Marshall came away profoundly impressed. He later remarked to Bradley: "There is a man who would make a wonderful instructor and I'll bet no one has asked for him." In fact, Bradley's official request for Smith to serve as an instructor in his weapons section had just reached Marshall's desk. The colonel found and read the request later in the day. "No words were exchanged between us," Bradley later recalled, "but I was elated. I had 'discovered'

Smith before he had!"[12] When Marshall completed his tour as assistant commandant at Benning—a tour extended beyond the customary four years, through the school year of 1931–1932—he did so with Bradley's name and record indelibly etched in his mind.

This was as Bradley hoped and intended it would be, but to Bradley's disappointment, Marshall did not leave Benning and immediately ascend to a position of great influence, a position from which he might have quickly shaped the course of his career. Instead, U.S. Army Chief of Staff Douglas MacArthur personally saw to it that Marshall was appointed senior instructor of the Illinois National Guard in Chicago, a position far from the military mainstream. In the fullness of time and in the exigency of a new world war, Marshall would come to occupy the very highest level of command and would not forget Omar Bradley. For now, however, as the close of Bradley's own tenure at the Infantry School drew near—it would end with the 1932–1933 term—he had to start thinking about making his next move, without the leveraging influence of Marshall or anyone else.

The most obvious step was enrollment in the Army War College, the loftiest of the army's professional schools. Yet the talk among the army's most promising mid-level officers—men like Bradley—was that War College graduates would never command troops in the next war. They would be assigned as headquarters and staff officers rather than line commanders. Stilwell, also slated to leave Benning at this time, intended to command troops, and accordingly refused to ask for assignment to the War College. He counseled Bradley to do the same. "Brad," he asked rhetorically, "why would you go to school to prepare yourself for a job you don't want?"[13]

It was true. Marshall himself had been assigned to Pershing's staff in France—and had been denied a field command—because he had had such an extensive staff education at Fort Leavenworth. Stilwell's argument was compelling, but that of Forest Harding—for Bradley a mentor of longer standing—was persuasive as well. Harding believed that the War College was playing an increasingly important role in the selection of general officers, and that, in any case, it was good background for any professional soldier. Stilwell could go his way, but, Harding let Bradley know, *he* was applying to the College.

Bradley was left torn between the advice of two officers he greatly admired, both of whom presented sound arguments. He had already been left out of one war, and did not wish to be excluded from combat command in another—should another come. On the other hand, if the War College was the gateway to a star or two . . .

In the end, Bradley settled the matter not by weighing the advice of others, no matter how valuable, but by reviewing his own experience. He concluded that each army school had helped him to grow professionally, and he believed that, if war came, he would somehow wrangle his way to troop duty. He therefore applied to the War College. Accepted, he was about to enjoy with his wife and daughter a long summer leave in Moberly before beginning classes. The increasingly harsh reality of a decade that was bringing economic hardship to America and warlike dictatorship to much of the rest of the world intervened, however. All leaves were summarily canceled as President Franklin D. Roosevelt called upon the U.S. Army to mobilize, organize, and lead some 300 thousand young unemployed men in the vast public works program known as the Civilian Conservation Corps (CCC).

In contrast to Bradley, who had grown up poor and Populist in Missouri, most of the army's officer corps was at least somewhat patrician, certainly conservative, and resolutely Republican. They resented having to deal with the CCC. Bradley, however, saw it as an opportunity to lead at least something resembling troops into something resembling rapid mobilization and even combat. After passing his summer in hard work rather than relaxation, Bradley reported in the fall of 1933 to Fort Humphreys (later renamed Fort McNair), home of the Army War College, on the banks of the Potomac River.

CHAPTER 6

From War College to War

As did many others who spent time in Washington between the wars, Omar Bradley described the capital as a sleepy city, slow and southern in pace and atmosphere. It was a most appropriate setting for the Army War College of the era, an institution that was neither warlike nor even very collegiate. When Bradley entered it in 1933, there were eighty-four students total, divided into teams of six or so, each team assigned a certain research topic. When a team felt that it had mastered the assigned material, its members made a presentation to the entire class. In contrast to the other army schools—especially the Infantry School under the Marshall regime—there was remarkably little pressure and no grading or evaluation of any kind. At one time, the War College created war plans for the General Staff. By 1933, it no longer served this function; students were not even allowed access to the actual plans the General Staff turned out for itself. War College's "war planning" was 100 percent hypothetical, built on data available to the man on the street: newspaper articles, magazine stories, books. There was very little realism in anything done at this, the pinnacle of the army's professional educational system. The group assigned to profile a rising German tyrant named Adolf Hitler concluded that he presented no threat on account of his obvious mental instability.

In Bradley's opinion, War College—the place where general officers were anointed—could best be characterized as irrelevant. As the anticlimax that was Bradley's War College year slipped by, its approaching end brought with it the usual question of where to go next. Simon Bolivar Buckner Jr., a colonel in 1934, destined to become a general in World War II and lead the tough, unheralded Aleutians campaign as well as the Tenth Army in Okinawa, was an old skeet-shooting partner. Having just been named commandant of cadets at West Point, he asked Bradley to consider teaching in the tactical department there. Mary was enthusiastic, especially since she knew that, as a senior major, her husband would merit first-class quarters. As always, teaching appealed to Bradley, who also felt that the position—in tactics—would be an opportunity to shape the development of a large number of future officers. His overall disappointment with the War College had more than persuaded him that the officer corps needed all the shaping and shaking up he could give it. He accepted Buckner's invitation.

<hr/>

By the time Bradley took up his new teaching post at the academy, the conservative, even reactionary regime of Fred Sladen, who had succeeded Douglas MacArthur as superintendent, had been replaced by that of Major General William D. Connor. MacArthur had succeeded John J. Pershing as army chief of staff, and Connor was MacArthur's handpicked man, who restored many of the reforms Superintendent MacArthur had himself originally introduced. Bradley felt that the academy was still rather hidebound, but at least its curriculum was more realistic. As an instructor in the tactical department (a so-called "tac") Bradley had the broadest possible teaching assignment: "to develop character, soldierly manhood, loyal discipline, gentlemanly conduct; to build physical strength, stamina and the coordination necessary for prolonged and arduous field service and to instruct every cadet in combat principles."[1]

In short, the academy's tacs taught cadets how to soldier, and among the fundamentals were weapons and small-unit maneuver, two areas that especially interested Bradley. Based on his experience as an Infantry School instructor, Bradley poured on the weapons training, with emphasis devoted to machine guns, mortars, and artillery—the weapons of increasing importance in modern infantry operations. He also applied his Hawaiian experience and made extensive use of detailed sand tables, or three-dimensional models of terrain. Bradley well understood that it was one thing to read a flat map, but quite another to develop a complete feel for actual terrain. His emphasis on developing a thorough knowledge of weapons technology and on learning to think of the battlespace in multiple dimensions was not only highly advanced for the 1930s but also became a foundation of professional military training in today's army.

Experience with the army's uneven schools had taught Omar Bradley one lesson above all others: The closer a student could be brought to the realities of war—the realities of movement, of combat, of logistics, of leadership, of technology—the better for the student and the better for the army. Pleased as he was that the West Point classroom experience had been made more practically meaningful than when he had been a cadet, Bradley believed that his best work as an academy instructor was done during the summer, outside of West Point's walls. New first classmen—the rising seniors of the academy—devoted their final summer touring actual military installations and observing maneuvers and weapons demonstrations. Cadets spent several weeks at Fort Benning (center of infantry activity) and Fort Monroe (center of coastal artillery and, far more important, anti-aircraft artillery development). The long-standing invisible wall separating the conventional army from the Army Air Corps was torn down, as cadets also spent two weeks at an air base. Bradley's advocacy of combined arms training and planning—the integration of infantry, armor, artillery, and air components—was at the leading edge of American military thought. Today it is a cornerstone of all American military doctrine.

From 1934 through 1938, Bradley mentored the generation of officers who would serve in junior commands during World War II and

Korea, then would rise to higher rank during the Vietnam and Cold War era. Five of his students became four-star generals, including Creighton W. Abrams Jr., Bruce Palmer Jr., Andrew J. Goodpaster Jr., John L. Throckmorton, and William Westmoreland. Westmoreland in particular recalled Bradley's pedagogical style: "quiet, sympathetic . . . , patient," yet frank and firm. During summer maneuvers in 1936, Westmoreland commanded a cadet battalion assigned to "defend" a hill. When the troops opposing him succeeded in taking the hill, Bradley, umpiring the maneuvers, summoned Westmoreland to his side.[2]

> "Mr. Westmoreland," he said, "look back at that hill. Look at it now from the standpoint of the enemy."
>
> Turning, I became aware for the first time of a concealed route of approach that it was logical for an attacker to use. Because I had failed to cover it with my defense, he as umpire had ruled for the attacking force.
>
> "It is fundamental," Major Bradley said calmly but firmly, "to put yourself always in the position of the enemy."[3]

Bradley was not interested in scolding Westmoreland, but in ensuring that he took away from the experience of defeat an element that would be key to victory: the principle of putting oneself in the place of the enemy. It is common to speak of great commanders—men like Napoleon Bonaparte or Robert E. Lee—as having possessed a genius for getting inside the mind of their opponent. Significantly, when Bradley counseled Cadet Westmoreland to put himself in the position of the enemy, he meant nothing so mystical. Instead, he brought Westmoreland literally to his opponent's position and invited him—again, literally—to *see* what the enemy saw and, from this perspective, to ponder the options available to him. As Bradley understood tactics, putting yourself in the enemy's physical position was a practical—not a mystical—means of getting inside his head. The exchange with Westmoreland was vintage Bradley, eliciting a principle of warfighting that is profound yet founded on the commonest of common sense.

Bradley also deliberately sought to bring something of "Marshall's Revolution" to West Point by streamlining and simplifying army routine and, even more important, developing officers capable of doing more than following orders. At the end of one summer camp, when the first classmen were preparing to dismantle the camp, one of Bradley's officers brought him an elaborate plan for the operation. It detailed precisely how each company tactical officer ("tac") would supervise every aspect of the dismantling. "I tore up the plan and said, 'No. I don't want a single officer in that camp. Turn it over to cadet officers. You can go over it later and see if they did it right. Let them learn to make decisions for themselves."[4] Typically of Bradley, he intended this episode to serve as a lesson in self-reliance not only to the cadets but to the tac officer who had drawn up the plan. Bradley wanted officers and non-comissioned officers to show initiative and creativity, but he also understood that, in order to elicit those qualities, the army needed a middle and senior level of command that both supported and demanded subordinates capable of making decisions for themselves. For Bradley, an army was not a by-the-book formation, but a team of individuals. He formed this attitude back when the army was very small, but it would remain unchanged when the army exploded into millions at the outbreak of World War II.

+≡≡+

In 1936, after a dozen years as a major, Bradley was promoted to lieutenant colonel. Shortly after his own promotion, Bradley learned that Colonel George C. Marshall, still commanding the Illinois National Guard, had finally been bumped up to brigadier general. It was doubtless a relief for Marshall, since he was overdue for the promotion. Had it been delayed further, he would almost certainly have been ineligible for further promotion at a later time, which would have meant that high command—including the position of chief of staff—would have been out of reach. Bradley himself must also have been relieved by Marshall's promotion, since he knew that his own prospects for advancement were at least loosely tied to those of his former commanding officer. He wrote Marshall a letter of congratulations, to which the inordinately reserved brigadier responded promptly. "His reply," Bradley wrote late in life, "is one of my most prized possessions":

I found your letter of congratulations on my return from leave. Thank you very much for writing as you did. I especially appreciate what you had to say, because you rank at the top among my Army contacts who have displayed the highest efficiency.

I very much hope we will have an opportunity to serve together again; I can think of nothing more satisfactory to me.[5]

For now, the prospect of a new assignment loomed as Bradley began the last year of his four-year West Point tour. Had his luck held, he would have moved up in this final year to the post of commandant of cadets; however, Connor, the superintendent under whom Bradley had served, was retiring, and the incoming superintendent, Brigadier General Jay L. Benedict, had another candidate in mind, Lieutenant Colonel Charles W. "Doc" Ryder, like Bradley a member of the Class of 1915. If Bradley was disappointed at being passed over as commandant of cadets, he did not let on. Nevertheless, it was clear that training and mentoring young officers agreed with him, and having been named commandant of cadets would have been a pleasure and a satisfaction.

In later years some writers would observe that I had the air of a schoolteacher. Perhaps this was not without good reason. Counting my one year at Brookings in South Dakota, my four years on the Fort Benning School staff and my two four-year tours at West Point, I was in fact officially a teacher for thirteen of my first twenty-three years of commissioned service. I might add that it is not a bad way to learn your profession thoroughly.[6]

But the time for teaching was running out. His four years as a West Point tac counted, as the army saw it, as a four-year tour "with troops." He had passed through all of the army's schools; there were none left. With school time and troop time behind him, the next move was obvious—and virtually mandatory. In 1938, Omar Bradley was ordered to serve on the War Department General Staff, Washington, D.C.

It was a critical time for such service. Adolf Hitler had just bloodlessly invaded Austria, summarily annexing it to his Third Reich in the *Anschluss*. The year before, Japan had invaded China—hardly without bloodshed—and the Sino-Japanese War was in its full fury. In grudging response to these developments, Congress authorized a modest expansion of the army and an increase in the size of the academy's Corps of Cadets, to 1,800.

The tentative approach Congress took to preparing for the possibility of war was reflected in the ambivalence that reigned at the highest level of the War Department. Franklin D. Roosevelt's secretary of war, Harry Woodring, was an isolationist, whereas his assistant secretary, Louis A. Johnson, was all for an aggressive program of rearmament. When the name of George C. Marshall came up as a possible replacement for General Malin Craig, who was slated to retire as chief of staff on September 1, 1939, Woodring and Johnson fell to arguing. Both agreed that Marshall was best qualified, but Woodring was reluctant to promote him over several more senior candidates. At the time, Marshall was chief of the War Department's War Plans Division and was clearly being readied to succeed General Stanley D. Embick as deputy chief of staff. Woodring leaned toward letting Marshall's upward progress take its natural course, moving him up to deputy when Embick retired and, in the meantime, appointing a more senior man as chief of staff. Johnson resolved the matter differently. Waiting until Woodring was temporarily absent from the office, he summarily ordered the outgoing Craig to relieve Embick and to name Marshall deputy chief of staff—immediately. Woodring returned to a done deal. The handwriting was now on the wall: Marshall was headed for the job of chief of staff, and Omar Bradley counted himself a disciple and protégé.

Bradley now took up his new assignment in G–1, the personnel division of what would become Marshall's General Staff. G–2 (intelligence) or G–3 (plans, training, and operations) would have been far more glamorous as General Staff assignments, at least in ordinary times. But these were not ordinary times. With each passing day, the war clouds over Europe became darker and more ominous. Bradley had reported to the War Department in June 1938. In September of that year, Hitler demanded a piece of Czechoslovakia, the German-speaking Sudentenland, and, by the end of the month, British prime minister Neville Chamberlain saw to it that he was given what he wanted. "Peace for our time," Chamberlain called the Munich Pact, by which he sought to "appease" Hitler, but

Bradley agreed with his General Staff colleagues that a European war with Hitler was now just a matter of time. And Congress, as well as the Roosevelt administration, seemed unmistakably to feel the same way. The army grew each year, significantly but still modestly: to 185 thousand by the spring of 1938, with plans for a 40 thousand-man increase during 1939. The rising numbers meant that G–1 was thrust into the forefront of General Staff activity, charged with smoothly and efficiently integrating the new officers and new men into the force. Brigadier General Lorenzo D. Gasser, G–1 chief, tapped Bradley to be his right hand as he responded to the orders of Craig and Marshall, who were in turn acting on secret instructions from FDR to proceed with the mobilization of the military for war. Upon the heads of the understaffed G–1 division an avalanche of paperwork fell, as Craig and Marshall called for one series of personnel mobilization plans after another, each keyed to a different set of scenarios and variables—especially varying levels of congressional funding. Bradley quickly learned to admire his commanding officer, General Gasser, who stubbornly refused to be overwhelmed.

<hr />

On April 27, 1939, Franklin D. Roosevelt officially announced his selection of George C. Marshall as the new chief of staff, effective July 1. One week after Marshall assumed his new duties, he walked into General Gasser's office. What happened next occurred (Bradley later recalled) "within my hearing"—although one wonders if Bradley, more anxious than he ever let on, was not above some deliberate eavesdropping.[7]

"I'm sorry," Marshall told Gasser, "but you've got one man in your section I want."

"I suppose you mean Bradley?"

"Yes."

The one person Marshall did not discuss the transfer with was Bradley himself, who followed orders to clean out his desk in G–1 and head down the hall to an anteroom in the suite occupied by the chief of staff.

As it turned out, Gasser was not long bereft of Bradley. Marshall radically reorganized the General Staff, generally streamlining—or simplifying—it. Very shortly after he took Bradley out of G–1, he took Gasser out of G–1 as well, naming him deputy chief of staff and assigning to him some three-fourths of all routine administrative business. Marshall saw his own job as promoting and planning rearmament and mobilization. The rest of the office work could be handled by the able Gasser. Marshall created a small inner staff dubbed the "secretariat," which functioned to evaluate the upward-flowing stream of paperwork flooding the chief of staff's office daily. The first function of the secretariat was to direct the flow, deciding which matters should go to Gasser and which required Marshall's personal attention. The second function of the secretariat was to reduce each paper it directed to Marshall to a single typewritten executive summary. Every day, members of the secretariat staff would orally present their summaries to Marshall, soliciting the chief's decision or action order. Bradley learned that the productive processing of information, like that of any other commodity, requires rational systems of logistics. From working closely with Marshall, Bradley became a great manager of data, a skill that helped make him a superb combat administrator. It was an essentially new command role, and Bradley became one of its pioneers.

Heading up the secretariat was Colonel Orlando Ward, who had graduated from the academy the year before Bradley and had seen service under Pershing both in Mexico, during the Punitive Expedition in pursuit of Pancho Villa, and in France during the Great War. Ward was allotted a pair of assistants and chose Lieutenant Colonel Stanley R. Mickelson, who combined expertise in anti-aircraft artillery and statistics, and Bradley. As Ward ran his little command, all three men were coequals, and all three were generally present when it was time to brief Marshall.

At first, the three men needed all the mutual support they could get. All were in awe of Marshall, who never passively received a briefing, but always asked sharply penetrating questions—to which, sometimes, no one had the answer. His response in such cases was disapproval by means of icy withdrawal. General Marshall never chewed anyone out, but the cold stare was enough to cut any subordinate down to size.

After a week of this treatment, Marshall summoned the secretariat into his office. "I'm disappointed in all of you," he said. An ashen-faced

Colonel Ward stammered in reply, "*Why*, sir?" Marshall explained: "You have not disagreed with anything I've done all week."[8]

Bradley grasped his meaning immediately and explained to Marshall that he had done nothing during the week with which they disagreed. He went on to assure the chief that, had one of his actions provoked disagreement, they would have spoken up. Marshall seemed unconvinced. Fortunately for the members of the secretariat, some days later a staff study passed through their hands, which was rife with problems. Their presentation to Marshall pointed out each flaw. On the verge of a smile, the chief said, "Now, *that's* what I want. Unless I hear all the arguments for or against an action I am about to take, I don't know whether or not I'm right. If I hear all the arguments against some action and still find in favor of it, I'm *sure* I'm right."[9]

For Bradley, it was an electrifying lesson in decision making. A commander did not solicit the advice of others in order to formulate his own decision, but used their advice to test the decision he had already made. If he could not be dissuaded from his decision, the rightness of the decision was affirmed. In this way, disagreement—not concord—was essential to the final phase of decision making.

Data management, workflow direction, the preparation of executive summaries, and playing devil's advocate were not the only roles Marshall assigned to his secretariat. Very often he handed them nearly impossible problems, demanding they be solved—instantly. Typical was the day on which Marshall gave Bradley a stack of papers, instructing him only to "Fix this."[10]

The top sheet of the stack laid out the problem: To alleviate a shortage of raw rubber, a vital strategic material threatened by growing Japanese aggression, rubber seeds would be shipped from menaced Southeast Asia for planting in Brazil under the auspices of FDR's hemispheric "Good Neighbor" Policy. It was a good idea at the time, until suddenly, the shipment had been stalled in Panama, and the seeds were in danger of spoiling. Bradley saw that Marshall had already penciled in a solution to the problem, writing at the bottom of the page: "Fly them to Brazil in B–17 bombers." But this "solution," he immediately grasped, was in itself a whole new problem—a "tall order . . . so tall I knew routine channels would be wholly inadequate."[11] Accordingly, he took the paper down the hall to the office of a Command and General Staff School classmate, Major General Henry H. "Hap" Arnold, freshly appointed deputy chief of staff for air. As usual, Arnold's outer office was jammed with others on urgent business, so Bradley, already an insider, slipped quietly through a back door that he knew to open directly into his classmate's office.

Presented with a problem, Bradley went about solving it by identifying the person with the power to solve it, then approached him by the most direct means available. These steps required wit, initiative, knowhow, and common sense. As soon as he walked into Arnold's office, Bradley realized that he had another factor on his side—a long familiar one: chance.

By sheer chance, Juan Trippe, CEO of Pan American World Airways and a pioneer of commercial aviation in the Pacific and Central and South America, was in conference with Arnold. Bradley interrupted the men, presented the problem, and received both the benefit of Trippe's extensive knowledge of airfield facilities in Brazil and Arnold's immediate cooperation in cutting orders to free up the necessary B–17s.

In the space of 20 minutes, Bradley had "fixed" what Marshall had ordered him to fix. "My reward for this performance was a grunt and a nod. [Marshall] expected no less of us."[12]

+≻═══≺+

The frenetic activity in the War Department and, in particular, the General Staff belied the lethargy that lingered over the nation as a whole, even as Hitler, Benito Mussolini, and the Japanese militarists continued their programs of conquest. The navy and the air arm received the lion's share of new funding, while the army was permitted to expand only in dribs and drabs and yet without the equipment and weapons necessary to keep pace with even this modest growth in personnel. When full-scale war burst upon Europe with the German invasion of Poland on September 1, 1939, Washington was dazed. The spectacle of blitzkrieg, the German invaders' "lightning war" across a quickly prostrated Poland, was nothing short of bewildering. A week after the invasion, FDR declared a "limited" state of national emergency, prompting Marshall to send a modified war alert to all army commands. The commanders acknowledged the alert and gave whatever orders were prescribed in the circumstance, yet, reading news accounts of the Polish invasion, U.S. military officers from the top down were as stunned as civilian Washington. The degree to which German forces had managed to coordinate air and ground assets, tanks and motorized infantry, was far in advance of anything the U.S. Army had ever conceived of, let alone possessed the capacity to implement. Bradley admitted it: "We were amazed, shocked, dumbfounded, shaking our heads in disbelief. Here was modern open warfare—war of maneuver—brought to the ultimate. To match such a performance, let alone exceed it, the U.S. Army had years of catching up and little time in which to do it."[13]

After the conquest of Poland and before the German invasion of the West began, the storm that was the blitzkrieg suddenly subsided, settling into what American newspapers called the "Phony War," a lull that lasted through the early spring of 1940. The alarm that had swept over civilian Washington likewise receded, even as the General Staff continued to draw up plans and budgets in anticipation of an all-out war. This was intensely demanding work for Bradley and the other members of the General Staff, but what made it much harder was the difficult position in which General George C. Marshall soon found himself. The long-simmering feud between Secretary of War Woodring and Assistant Secretary of War Johnson exploded as Johnson conducted an unseemly press campaign to undercut Woodring and thereby effect a departmental coup d'etat. The result, however, was neither the immediate downfall of Woodring nor the elevation of Johnson, but the utter paralysis of the civilian leadership of the War Department at a critical time in history. Already the senior army authority in uniform, Marshall was now obliged also to assume leadership tasks that were rightly the province of the army secretary. This he was willing to do, but he was acutely aware that he did not yet enjoy the full confidence of the White House and that Congress barely knew him. For these reasons, Marshall believed it would be folly to present what his staff had been working on—a blue-sky budget for full-scale mobilization. Instead, he returned to his staff and directed them to prepare, as it were, another set of books, these reflecting modest budget demands that would have a reasonable chance for immediate passage. Marshall had no doubt that Hitler would get moving again in Europe, and when that happened, he would return to the president and Congress with a much larger request. For now, though, it was best to play it conservatively.

Marshall was, of course, right about Hitler. Blitzkrieg came to the Western Front in April 1940. Denmark, Norway, and the Low Countries quickly fell, smashed up, as Winston Churchill wrote to President Roosevelt, "like matchwood."[14] With its Maginot Line, formidable army, substantial air force, and world-class navy, France was expected to make an effective stand, especially with the help of Great Britain. But the British Expeditionary Force (BEF) was driven out of France by the end of May, barely escaping more or less intact via Dunkirk, and France surrendered to Germany on June 22. With the English under grave threat, the mood throughout the United States—from the politicians to the people—shifted, again as Marshall had predicted it would. Marshall set his hard-pressed staff to work preparing far more ambitious budgets, and, equally important, President Roosevelt cleaned house among the civilian leadership of the War Department, ousting both Woodring and Johnson and bringing in the extraordinarily capable Henry Stimson, former secretary of war under William Howard Taft, as *his* secretary of war. Seventy-two years old but still in full vigor of mind and energy, Stimson revitalized the War Department's civilian component. It was high time.

+══─═══+

The fall of France roused America from its long sleep. In August 1940, Congress enacted legislation calling up the National Guard and, on September 16, passed the Selective Service Act, authorizing the first peacetime military draft in American history. In 1938, the influx of new troops had been a trickle, and in 1939 a steadier flow; beginning the fall of 1940, it became a flood, overwhelming the administration of the army, which lacked the means of assimilating so many so fast. Drowning in the administrative chaos and with Europe ablaze, Omar Bradley longed to get out of the office and into a field command.

As 1940 drew to a close, Bradley glimpsed a way out of the staff and toward the troops. Brigadier General Robert L. Eichelberger, recently appointed superintendent of West Point, visited the General Staff and chatted with Bradley as the two waited for Marshall in his outer office.

Almost casually, Eichelberger asked: "How'd you like to be commandant of cadets?"[15]

It was the job for which he had been passed over in the final year of his second West Point tour, but Bradley did not quite jump at it. From his current position, relieving "Doc" Ryder as commandant would be perceived as a step down or, viewed more charitably, as a lateral move. It certainly did not merit a promotion. Nevertheless, it *was* a step out of staff work and in the direction of troop command—indeed, as the army saw it, commanding the academy's tactical department and the Corps of Cadets *was* a troop command. At the very least, Bradley would be influencing men who would be combat company commanders in the coming war, and, at best, the position would be a stepping stone to an actual combat command for himself.

After mulling it for several minutes, Bradley replied that he would like very much to be commandant of cadets. The wheels were put into motion, and Marshall approved the transfer. Some days later, however, he summoned Bradley into his office to ask him if he was sure he wanted to go to West Point. Bradley replied by rehearsing his reasons for accepting the job. Marshall "glanced idly out the window and then said, 'How'd you like to have Hodges' job?'"[16]

Brigadier General Courtney Hodges commanded the Infantry School at Fort Benning. This time, not even a few minutes' mulling was required. Here was an opportunity to shape—to shape directly—how the coming war would be fought. Bradley snapped at the offer. He would go to Benning, not West Point.

———◆———

Bradley arrived at Fort Benning on February 25, 1941, and found a telegram from the War Department waiting for him. He had been jumped from lieutenant colonel to brigadier general, passing over the grade of colonel entirely. With a certain exhilaration, he took note that he was the first of the Class of 1915 to get a star. He took even more pride in having been chosen to relieve Courtney Hodges, who for years "had been to me an august figure like Marshall and a man I admired almost equally."[17]

As Bradley took up his duties at the Infantry School, army strength stood at more than one half-million men, with a force of 1.4 million called for by the end of June. This was to include about 100 thousand officers of all grades. Most of the army brass had blithely assumed that the National Guard and Reserve would furnish a sufficient number of officers to meet the demand. As usual, the prescient Marshall dissented from his colleagues. He believed that most of the junior officers in the National Guard would be inadequately trained or in other ways unsuited to Regular Army command, while the Reserve officers would be needed in such non-infantry roles as the Air Corps. At the very least, there would be a critical shortage of infantry officers. Marshall therefore proposed the establishment of new army schools for the rapid training of junior officers to be commissioned directly from the enlisted ranks and even from top-performing incoming draftees after they had passed through six months of basic training. Marshall's own G–1 chief opposed the creation of these "Officer Candidate Schools" (OCSs), and the prototype OCS that Hodges established at Fort Benning—mainly to placate Marshall—was a puny and half-hearted effort, with just two poorly organized, poorly led classes. In contrast to Hodges, Bradley embraced the OCS idea and immediately drew up what he characterized as "a sort of assembly-line plan," which would expand the OCS program at Benning by a factor of 24 "without exorbitant expense or the need for large numbers of skilled instructors."[18] Bradley took the plan to Washington, where it met stiff resistance from established officers, who disparaged OCS graduates as "ninety-day wonders." Frustrated through established channels, Bradley executed an end run around them and took his plan directly to Marshall, who approved it immediately.

Under Bradley, Fort Benning became the pilot and the model OCS for the many that were established throughout the army in World War II. Bradley considered the OCS program to be his most important contribution to the mobilization effort, and to this day he is justly called the father of OCS.

As commandant of the Infantry School, Bradley also sought to redress the institution's failure to develop and teach strategy and tactics that integrated air operations and mechanized warfare into infantry doctrine. He championed the formation and training of air combat units, both for close air support of infantry and for airborne assault using paratroops and glider troops. He was also an enthusiastic advocate of mechanization and armor, believing that the proper role for tanks exploited their mobility to the fullest, which meant coordinating them with infantry operations, but not—as was the conventional and prevailing view—subordinating them to infantry. Tanks, Bradley saw, were best used as offensive assets, whereas most of his infantry colleagues advocated their use in more or less defensive (covering) support of infantry. Bradley believed that it was a foolish waste of the high-speed potential of mechanization to compel mobile forces to conform to the relatively slow pace of soldiers moving on foot.

Among those who agreed passionately with Bradley's point of view was George S. Patton Jr., the driving force behind the creation of the 2nd Armored Division, which was already established at Fort Benning when Bradley arrived. For about a year, Bradley and Patton worked closely together at Benning. It was here that Bradley's original distaste for Patton rapidly evolved into a complex of attraction and revulsion. Patton's bravura performance in the army's ambitious Tennessee, Louisiana-Texas, and Carolina maneuvers during 1941 made it clear, Bradley believed, "that we had on our hands one of the most extraordinary fighting generals the Army has ever produced." Yet he was never able really to understand Patton, whom he characterized as "the most fiercely ambitious man and the strangest duck" he had ever known. Bradley discerned that Patton was "motivated by some deep, inexplicable martial spirit," which he fed with omnivorous reading in military history and martial poetry. As for the men of Patton's command, Bradley believed he was much too hard on them, so that most both respected and despised him. His social grace and disarming charm did not escape Bradley, but neither did his "macho profanity," which Bradley thought was "unconscious overcompensation for . . . a voice that was almost comically squeaky and high-pitched, altogether lacking in command authority."[19]

Perhaps most of all, Bradley disapproved of Patton's overweening vanity. No doubt he was a great fighting general, but he refused to concern himself with details, especially dull but crucial logistics.[20]

Despite Bradley's heavy freight of ambivalence about Patton, he was sorry to part company with him when Patton moved his training center to the California desert. For the rest of his professional life, Bradley acknowledged that he had learned a great deal about mechanized warfare from Patton, and, for his part, Patton seems not to have picked up on any of Bradley's doubts about him—at least not during his time at Benning. "During our service together," he wrote to Bradley after he left for California, "I never was associated with anyone who more whole-heartedly and generously cooperated with everything we worked on together."[21]

⊹⇌⇌⊹

Late in 1941, General Marshall came to Fort Benning on one of several visits he made during Bradley's tenure there. He turned to Bradley and asked bluntly: "Bradley, do you have a man to take your place when you leave here to command a division?" Bradley could hardly catch his breath. Divisions, he knew, were going to much more senior officers. Divisional command, "the epitome for an infantry officer," meant another star, and Bradley had been a brigadier for just six months.[22]

After Marshall concluded his visit, Bradley began preparing Colonel Leven C. "Lev" Allen to take his place as commandant of the Infantry School while he awaited the activation of a division he would command. On one Sunday afternoon during this period—it was December 7, 1941—Bradley and his wife were cleaning up a flowerbed in the yard behind their Fort Benning quarters. Harold R. "Pink" Bull, an old friend who was now working for Bradley as an instructor in logistics, walked up to the couple. His wife, Betty, was with him.

Have you heard the news? Bull asked. *The Japanese bombed Pearl Harbor.*

"I immediately put on my uniform and hurried to post headquarters . . ."[23]

CHAPTER 7

In Africa

Some days after Pearl Harbor, before the end of December, Lieutenant Colonel George van Wyck Pope, a friend from the West Point faculty and now in G–1 (personnel) at the War Department, telephoned Omar Bradley. Three new divisions were being activated from scratch: the 77th, 82nd, and 85th. Bradley was to take command of the 82nd and receive a temporary promotion to major general.

It was a thrill but also a formidable challenge. Created during World War I, the 82nd quickly compiled a storied battle record, fighting in all the major engagements to which the American Expeditionary Force (AEF) had been committed. In a war that produced few universally familiar names for Americans, the 82nd was renowned for its sharpshooting, Medal of Honor-winning sergeant from the Tennessee backwoods, Alvin C. York, whose story had been retold by Hollywood just months before Pearl Harbor with Gary Cooper in the title role. Its fame notwithstanding, the 82nd had been deactivated shortly after the armistice, and the resurrected division was to be a bold experiment in rapid mobilization. Traditionally, conscripts were sent into established outfits in the National Guard or Regular Army. The need for expansion was now so urgent, however, that the army decided to create the new 82nd virtually overnight by building it out of draftees organized around a small cadre of experienced officers and enlisted men. The latter would constitute just 10 percent of the division (700 officers, 1,200 enlisted men, including noncoms), and the former—green inductees all—90 percent: 16 thousand men sent directly from their induction centers.

Bradley was keenly aware that the potential for catastrophic failure was high. Training would be a daunting task, but he knew how to train soldiers. The more serious problem, Bradley decided, was morale. He understood that "an army draftee's most desolate hours occurred on arrival. Only a few days away from home, family and loved ones, cast into a strange, impersonal and wholly unfamiliar world, senselessly ordered to 'hurry up and wait,' for this seemingly stupid reason or that, it was no wonder than depression and homesickness were commonplace." In the traditional division, which integrated a few newcomers into an established outfit, the impact these emotions had on collective morale was significant, but manageable. But "with an entire division of new draftees reporting to an organization that did not even exist except on paper, there was real danger that we might experience devastating morale problems" that would impede training and readiness and even undermine public and political confidence in the army. [1]

Bradley conceived what he called the radical idea to "do everything within our ability to make the draftees feel they were coming to a 'home' where people really cared about their welfare." He did not intend to "coddle the recruits"—but to "be tough as hell on them . . . in an intelligent, humane, understanding way." Even as the officers of the 82nd were to be coached in transforming assignment to the division as a kind of homecoming, they were also instructed to build on the 82nd's illustrious history, so that the draftees would feel that they were "not only coming to a home, but a famous, even elitist, one." [2]

Nor was Bradley's "radical" program exclusively an exercise in feel-good psychology. Always the eminently practical soldier, Bradley took concrete, tangible, practical steps toward inculcating the feelings he wanted to pervade his command. He detailed his adjutant, Ralph P. "Doc" Eaton, to send G–1 teams to reception centers in Georgia, Alabama, Mississippi, and Tennessee (the states from which most of the division's conscripts came) to welcome, interview, and classify each draftee with an eye toward matching the man to the job. Those who had been truck drivers in civilian life would be put down for motor pool duty, short-order cooks assigned to the mess, file clerks to company offices, and so on. When the men showed up at Camp Claiborne, the division's home outside of Alexandria, Louisiana, there was a place and a job for each of them. As they stepped off the train, Bradley had a brass band waiting on the platform to welcome them. Since the G–1 teams had already placed them, they were told precisely where to go, and they found their assigned tents fully furnished with all required equipment and bedding. From here, it was to the mess tent and a hot meal. Everything was thought of, down to a special rush laundry service, which allowed the newcomers to refresh the uniforms they had traveled in. Just as Bradley's Benning Officer Candidate School (OCS) became the model for OCSs throughout the army, so his reception system was recommended to all new divisions. Today, both morale and intelligent job placement are top priorities for army personnel managers. Like Bradley in World War II, they are not content to leave these issues to chance.

Bradley's reception system did much to soften the shock experienced by incoming draftees, but, for commanders, the "rudest shock . . . was the discovery that [the draftees], the prime youth of America, were generally in appallingly poor physical condition." Bradley instituted a rigorous program of physical training, which included daily calisthenics and sports, as well as a formidable obstacle course. He ordered everyone in the division, officers and men, to participate in the fitness program and did not except himself. Indeed, Bradley took pride in running the obstacle course—although that pride was somewhat tarnished when, a month after his 49th birthday, his hands slipped on the rope swing, and he "fell, very un-Tarzan-like, into a stinking raw sewage drainage ditch beneath it." Matthew Ridgway remarked that the "sight of a two-star general in such a predicament was a vast delight to all ranks."[3]

At the end of 17 weeks, Bradley was confident that he had forged the 82nd into a combat-ready division, and he looked forward to leading it into battle. But just as he was completing the training cycle, he received War Department orders summarily transferring him to command of the 28th National Guard Division, a unit, he was told, that needed help badly.

Eighteen National Guard divisions were mobilized during 1940–1941, with uniformly poor results. Officers were overage and generally unfit, especially at the highest ranks, where they were often the equivalent of the Civil War's "political generals," commanders chosen by virtue of "old-boy" political connections rather than military qualifications. Because the officers were inadequate, the enlisted ranks were even worse. The 28th was typical, and Bradley assumed that he had been chosen not only to fix it, but, in fixing this unit, to provide a model for the other Guard divisions.

The division had been called up in January 1941 and passed through basic training in its native Pennsylvania before shipping out to Camp Livingston, Louisiana, just ten miles from Alexandria. For their first four weeks at Camp Livingston, Bradley and his staff closely studied the problems of the 28th. The most obvious was that the division was being routinely raided by other units for manpower, leaving it critically short of officers and noncoms. Almost worse was a condition Bradley dubbed "home-townism": "A unit commander from Podunk would have in his outfit . . . sons of his home-town banker on whom he was professionally dependent in civilian life. He might be hesitant to properly discipline the sons."[4] At the very least, home-townism bred favoritism, which made it impossible to create a truly effective organization. Against arguments that, in armies all over the world, regiments were routinely raised from particular localities, a practice that enhanced the cohesiveness of a unit, Bradley summarily transferred all of the division's officers and noncoms to new companies, with no two noncoms going to the same outfit. Fearing that the shake-up might stir a mutiny, Bradley was pleasantly surprised when it was met instead with universal approval

As in the 82nd, physical fitness was also an issue, and Bradley ordered a series of "work-up" hikes culminating in a twenty-five-mile hike, which he completed along with his men. Under Bradley, the 28th National Guard Division became a tough fighting outfit. Shortly after New Year 1943, the 28th was moved to Camp Gordon Johnson at Carrabelle, Florida, for amphibious assault training, an experience that gave Bradley profound respect for the tactical and logistical problems entailed in amphibious assault. It was an introductory lesson in a subject for which the final exam would be D-Day, June 6, 1944.

+====+

With the 28th not only rehabilitated, but rendered combat ready, Bradley received a telegram on February 16 elevating him to command of X Corps, based at Temple, Texas, near Austin. No sooner had he read the message than the telephone rang. General Lesley J. McNair's G–1, Alexander Bolling, was on the other end of the line.[5]

"We're cutting orders for you today, Brad. You're going on extended active duty. Not the division—just you."

Flabbergasted, Bradley stammered, "I've just received orders to Temple, Texas, to—"

"Oh, that was yesterday," Bolling replied, cutting him off.

Composing himself as best he could, Bradley managed to ask: "Well, what kind of clothes? Which way do I go?"

Bolling understood that he wanted to know whether he was bound for Africa or the Pacific. He could not answer directly on an open telephone line, so he replied, simply: "Remember your classmate? You're going to join him."

Bradley knew that the classmate in question was Dwight D. Eisenhower, commander-in-chief of Allied forces in the Mediterranean theater, which, at present, was fighting in North Africa.

"How soon can you leave?" Bolling asked. "You'll have to be briefed in Washington."

Now in full control of his emotions, Bradley replied: "Tomorrow."

+====+

Bradley's elation at finally being sent into combat quickly faded as he began to realize that he was not being given a specific troop command in

Africa, but instead was being assigned to some unspecified job. Bradley suspected that the corps command dangled briefly before him had been yanked away, and that Marshall had now earmarked him for a position on Ike's staff, perhaps the equivalent of the function Marshall himself had served in Pershing's headquarters during World War I.

With profound misgivings, Bradley headed to Washington, where he reported directly to General George C. Marshall. During Bradley's absence from the General Staff, the War Department had moved from its shabbily quaint quarters in the Munitions Building on Constitution Avenue to the newly completed behemoth known as the Pentagon. Marshall received his former staffer, sat him down, and devoted no more than ten minutes to outlining his mission in Africa. Bradley would later write: "All I learned . . . was that I was to serve in some vague capacity on the Tunisian front," at Eisenhower's discretion.[6]

At the time of Operation Torch, which had landed U.S. forces in North Africa on November 8, 1942, the French colonies were ostensibly loyal to Vichy, which meant that they were enemies of the British and Americans. But Eisenhower managed to win them over—at least to the extent of limiting armed opposition in some places, removing it altogether in others, and even securing an actual military alliance in still other parts of the theater. Although it was infinitely better not to be facing French bullets along with Italian and German ones, the ex-Vichy administrators of the French colonies remained unreliable at best and troublesome at worst. Toward the British, the French were downright hostile. And, eager to exploit the general instability was a combination of Arab nationalists and Arab tribalists, both craving freedom from their colonial bonds. Some in North Africa regarded Ike and his armies as liberators, others as invaders. Eisenhower had to conduct his campaign against the German and Italians, ever fearful that Frenchmen or Arabs would join forces with them.

Enemies and former enemies presented a difficult enough challenge. Added to this were the dealings with America's supposedly bosom ally, the British. American officers distrusted their British counterparts, and the British commanders were generally contemptuous of American officers and fighting men alike.

They had reason to be. Against Rommel—the "Desert Fox"—neither the British nor the Americans were performing well, and at Kasserine

Pass in Tunisia, the inexperienced American troops broke completely on February 20, 1943, allowing Rommel to advance through their defensive position. It was the first major battle between a U.S. and a German force, and it was a humiliating defeat for the Americans. Ike had somehow to get his arms around the deteriorating situation, and he needed a good set of eyes and ears on the front, which was spread out over some 1,200 miles, from Casablanca on the Atlantic coast east to Tunisia. Ike sent Marshall a list of thirteen candidates for the job, including Bradley. "The nature of the work involved here," Eisenhower wrote, "requires brains, tact and imagination more than it does thorough acquaintanceship with the theater."[7] Out of Ike's list, Marshall chose Bradley, and Eisenhower enthusiastically agreed.

After a 90-hour trip on a succession of Air Transport Command aircraft, a weary Bradley and his two aides landed in Algiers on February 24. They were driven in Eisenhower's bulletproof Cadillac staff car to his headquarters at the St. George Hotel. Twenty-eight years earlier, Ike had written an admiring portrait of his West Point classmate in *The Howitzer,* the academy yearbook, but they had seen very little of one another since. Nevertheless, Ike greeted Bradley "warmly and effusively, like a long-lost brother," making him feel instantly "at home—and needed."[8] He gave Bradley a detailed briefing, leaving the newcomer profoundly impressed with his detailed grasp of the battlefield situation and his willingness to accept total responsibility for the reverses the Allies had suffered, including the humiliation of Kasserine. The only hint of extenuation was Ike's criticism of his G–2 (intelligence officer), British brigadier general Eric E. Mockler-Ferryman, who had put blind faith in Ultra decrypts.

At this time, "Ultra" was the name that British intelligence applied to all decrypts of German coded communications. The origin of the term was the designation of code breaking as a secret so secret that it was beyond "top secret," thus, *ultra* secret. For an officer to be "put into the Ultra picture," to be granted access to the decrypts, was to be admitted into the equivalent of an elite Masonic society. Perhaps in part for this reason, intelligence derived from Ultra decrypts was almost universally regarded as beyond impeachment or even critical questioning. Many commanders believed that to possess Ultra information was to have a window into the German military mind. Naturally skeptical, Bradley also had the good fortune to arrive in theater just after a major failure of Ultra intelligence. He therefore entered the war with what he characterized as a very cautious attitude toward this so-called unimpeachable intelligence. Bradley put a high premium a combat intelligence, but he never relied on single stream of information. He would come to value Ultra, but he always sought corroboration.

Following the briefing, Ike handed Bradley his formal orders. His assignment was not only to serve as Eisenhower's eyes and ears on the Tunisian front, reporting to Ike directly, but also to "make 'suggestive changes' (as Ike put it) to American commanders at the front." [9] Having journeyed four days and nights from Washington to get into the war, it seemed to Bradley that he was being saddled with an odious mission that had failure written all over it. It was bad enough that he would be perceived at the front as a spy for Ike—a dangerous, morale-busting abridger of the chain of command—but, even worse, he, an outsider new to the region and new even to combat, was charged with telling front-line commanders how to fight the war. Bradley resolved to go about his risky business as quietly, inconspicuously, and unobtrusively as possible.

Thus Major General Omar Nelson Bradley arrived in Africa not to fight there, but to evaluate everything and everyone. He began with Ike himself, finding much to admire, but also coming away convinced that he had become slavishly pro-British in his thinking. On February 27, Bradley flew to Constantine, Algeria, where British general Harold Alexander, Eisenhower's deputy commander, had his headquarters. Bradley was duly impressed, finding Alexander to be charming and shrewd, possessed of a firm strategic grasp of the entire theater. He had lost patience with both of his senior commanders in Tunisia, Lloyd Fredendall, who, as commander of the U.S. II Corps, had presided over the disaster at Kasserine Pass, and British general Sir Kenneth Arthur Anderson, a Scotsman as taciturn, sour, argumentative, and pessimistic as he was personally courageous.

Alexander had so far been unsuccessful in his efforts to persuade Eisenhower to replace Fredendall and General Bernard Law Montgomery to replace Anderson, and Bradley left Constantine convinced that, whatever the actual merits and flaws of Fredendall and Anderson, it boded ill that Ike's deputy, his main man on the ground, had lost confidence in them both. Heavy with concern, Bradley, in company with his two aides and Ike's chief of staff Walter Bedell "Beetle" Smith, jeeped it from Constantine to their next stop, Fredendall's II Corps headquarters at Djebel Kouif, a Tunisian village some 15 miles north of Tebessa.

Like everyone who comes to the Tunisian desert, Bradley was shocked by the pervasive, bone-chilling cold. He was even more appalled by the reception Fredendall accorded him, which was even colder. Although he had quartered himself in a comfortable home, Fredendall did not invite Bradley and Smith to share it, banishing them instead to a shabby and windowless hotel. If Bradley was concerned about Ike's tendency to defer to the British, he was now far more worried by the attitude of Fredendall and his II Corps staff, who "were rabidly, if not obscenely, anti-British and especially anti-Anderson."[10] To put it mildly, this was no way to forge an effective alliance. Both Bradley and Smith recommended that Eisenhower relieve Fredendall.

Bradley did not confine his tour to the topmost tier of command. Braving the cold rain, he visited each of the four U.S. divisions of II Corps. He got an earful from his West Point friend and former boss on Marshall's secretariat, Orlando Ward, who commanded 1st Armored Division, II Corps. The division, he said, had been divided among the Americans, Free French, and British and had never been allowed to fight as a unit. Worse, Fredendall seized personal command of some of the division's units, and when those units collapsed under Rommel's onslaught, he blamed Ward, demanding that Ike relieve him. Instead, Eisenhower dispatched Ernest Harmon, one of Bradley's War College classmates, to serve as something Ike called a "useful senior assistant." The desperate Fredendall simply turned over battle command to Harmon and retired from the field, inducing in Harmon such disgust that he recommended Fredendall's relief and reported to Patton that the II Corps commander was a "physical and moral coward."[11]

After visiting Ward's armored division, Bradley called on II Corps' three infantry divisions. Two of the commanders—Lieutenant Colonel Charles W. "Doc" Ryder (34th National Guard Infantry Division) and Terry de la Mesa Allen (1st Infantry Division, the "Big Red One")—he knew well, considering both courageous as well as skilled tactical leaders. When they placed the blame for the defeat at Kasserine Pass on

Fredendall, Bradley believed them—but he did not gloss over what he saw as a very real problem with Allen. Like his second in command, the colorful Brigadier General Theodore Roosevelt Jr. (son of former President Teddy Roosevelt), Allen was a dashing leader well loved by his men, but a commander unwilling and apparently unable to instill military discipline in a division that had developed a loose, devil-may-care cockiness: plenty of morale, but precious little collective efficiency.

As for the commander of the 3rd Infantry Division, Manton S. Eddy, Bradley did not know him personally, but he was immediately impressed by his evident professionalism, despite an inclination to an excess of caution.

For whatever reason, despite a growing list of complaints, Eisenhower had long resisted relieving Lloyd Fredendall. When Ike arrived in person at Fredendall's headquarters on March 5, he drew Bradley aside.

"What do you think of command here?"

"Pretty bad," was Bradley's laconic reply.

That's all it finally took. "Thanks, Brad," Ike said. "You've confirmed what I thought."[12]

<hr />

Bradley's assessment corroborated the opinions of Alexander, Anderson, and Harmon as well as Lucian Truscott and Walter Bedell Smith, so that by the time Eisenhower decided to relieve Fredendall he already had chosen his replacement: George Smith Patton Jr. Though Patton was slated to lead the newly created Seventh U.S. Army in Operation Husky, the invasion of Sicily, Eisenhower decided that he could first be employed to do everything possible to rehabilitate II Corps. It was a bold gamble on Ike's part. He believed that the flamboyant and fiery Patton was more likely than any other commander to succeed in putting iron in the II Corps spine, but he was also aware that Patton lacked the tact and diplomacy to get on with the British. He therefore decided to recommend to Patton that he take on Bradley—calm, quiet, diplomatic—as his deputy commander. Not only would this serve to moderate Patton's more volatile tendencies, it would also break Bradley into combat command, blooding the 50-year-old soldier and giving Ike an opportunity to see how his "eyes and ears" performed as a battle leader. If he passed muster as Patton's "understudy"—the term was Bradley's own—he would take over II Corps when Patton returned to planning Operation Husky.

Insofar as an "understudy" is supposed to learn from the star of the show, the self-applied label was accurate enough, but to the degree that the term implied slavish emulation, it was not. Bradley was convinced that "Patton was a superb field general and leader—perhaps our very best," but his "many human and professional flaws . . . held the potential for . . . disaster." He watched as Patton roared into II Corps headquarters in a scout car with wailing siren and blaring klaxon horn and how he instituted a strict spit-and-polish dress code, including the celebrated "necktie order" that mandated the wearing at all times of helmets, leggings, freshly laundered and pressed uniforms—and neckties. He watched as Patton insisted that every man under his command perfect a military salute so smartly distinctive that the "Patton salute" soon came to distinguish everyone associated with a Patton outfit. He stood by as Patton made dramatic appearances in unlikely places to deliver exuberantly profane pep talks. Bradley watched, and was not amused. He found Patton's approach "excessively harsh" and believed that a "firm but more mature and considerate discipline would no doubt have achieved the same results."[13]

The fact was that by the time both Patton and Bradley assumed command of II Corps, the crisis in Tunisia was over. Montgomery's Eighth British Army had Rommel on the ropes, U.S. forces were now in good order, and Allied air and naval assets had essentially confined the Germans and Italians to the Tunisian peninsula. There was little question that victory was readily within the Allies' grasp. The only open issue was how to defeat a trapped enemy quickly and devastatingly, allowing as few troops to escape as possible.

By this time, Rommel had lost all faith in the possibility of victory and urged immediate withdrawal with an eye toward rapid evacuation in order to preserve the army intact. Neither Adolf Hitler nor Benito Mussolini would, however, hear of such a thing, and they ordered Rommel to make a stand and conduct an all-out campaign to the death. In the end, for Rommel personally, the order was moot. Plagued by a number of illnesses, he turned over command to Jürgen von Arnim on March 9 and returned to Germany.

Of course, none of this was known to the Allies. Had it been, General Alexander's pervasive pessimism—he still had no confidence in American military leaders or American fighting men—might not have moved him to formulate his excessively cautious approach to the final defeat of the Axis in North Africa. Instead of boldly attacking, using II Corps to drive a wedge between German forces in the north and south, he advocated using the Eighth British Army to squeeze the Afrika Korps from the south, pushing it relentlessly north back into Tunis. In the meantime, the First Army, under Anderson, would simply hold the central and northern portions of the front in Tunis while II Corps would do no more than support these British-led operations by making a feinting attack in the southern sector of the front intended to relieve pressure that would otherwise be applied against the Eighth and First Armies.

Whereas Patton bitterly protested being cast into so subordinate a role, Bradley expressed nothing more than mild disappointment. The fact was that he at least partially agreed with Alexander's judgment that II Corps was not ready to bear the full responsibility of offensive battle and thought it better to ease the unit into combat. For better or worse, Omar Bradley was a commander who appreciated nuance. The hard-riding cavalryman Patton characteristically went for broke, sometimes slighting logistics, often leaving flanks exposed. His audacity terrified Allied high command almost as much as it shook the Germans. In contrast, the infantryman Bradley was far more methodical and measured in his approach to combat. Bradley was certainly frustrated by Montgomery's habitually excessive thoroughness in preparing for the British-led attack Alexander had authorized, yet he managed to find the delay useful insofar as it provided more time for him and Patton to hone II Corps.

At last, on March 17, 1943, II Corps went into action. Its 1st Infantry Division—the "Big Red One"—under Terry de la Mesa Allen was tasked with capturing Gafsa and then El Guettar, which was to serve as a supply and fuel dump for Montgomery's principal offensive. The 1st Armored Division, under Orlando Ward, was to advance eastward through Kasserine Pass, taking Station de Sened, northeast of El Guettar, then to occupy the high ground in the vicinity of Maknassy. The 9th Infantry Division—greenest of the II Corps outfits, under Eddy—would contribute forces to the 1st Infantry and 1st Armored Divisions as needed, while "Doc" Ryder's 34th Division was held in reserve against the possibility of an Axis retreat in its direction.

Although these operations were subordinate to Montgomery's big show, they were a make-or-break opportunity to redeem II Corps and, with it, the prestige of the U.S. Army in Africa. Alexander as well as Eisenhower were guests at the corps' advanced headquarters in Feriana when the operation got under way. Patton then left to accompany Allen in the advance on Gafsa while Bradley joined Ward's assault toward Station de Sened.

It was the first time Omar Bradley heard shots fired in anger, but that is not what nearly killed him within the opening hours of battle. His jeep rolled over an Italian landmine. Charged with eight sticks of dynamite, it proved to be a dud, but Bradley admitted to being so "unnerved by this close call [that] it required considerable effort not to show it."[14]

Allen's Big Red One quickly captured Gafsa, then barreled down on El Guettar. Ward's 1st Armored also easily took its first objective, Station de Sened, but heavy rains then churned the thirsty desert into a quagmire, which bogged down the heavy tanks as they struggled toward the Maknassy high ground. Enraged by his lack of progress, Patton excoriated Ward, accusing him of being gun-shy after Kasserine Pass. As Bradley saw it, the weather, not Ward, was to blame for the slowdown, but Patton would hear none of it, and Bradley concluded that Ward was doomed to lose his command. The predicament of the 1st Armored Division was intensified by Montgomery's own problems, as his frontal assault was stymied by unexpectedly tenacious German resistance. Patton believed that if he could get 1st Armored moving, II Corps could ride to Monty's rescue—a scenario he relished as much for the humiliation it would cause the British commander as for what it would do to the enemy. But, although Patton railed against him, Ward was unable to move ahead.

Fortunately for Patton, Montgomery, and the reputation of the American army, Terry Allen's assault on El Guettar was far more successful. It drew a counterattack by two Axis divisions on March 23, which Allen managed to turn into an ambush, savaging the Italians and

Germans, thereby achieving the U.S. Army's first substantial victory against an Axis force and redeeming the honor of II Corps.

The Big Red One's victory should also have gone far to inculcate among the British confidence in American arms; however, Alexander showed no inclination to alter his plan for the final conquest of Tunisia, which, with the exception of Eddy's 9th Infantry, totally excluded II Corps. This time, Bradley partook wholly of Patton's outrage, but whereas Patton felt personally barred from glory, Bradley believed that "our troops had won the right, and we owed it to the American people, to share in the final victory."[15] When Montgomery's offensive faltered, Bradley secured Patton's permission to fly to Algiers to protest the long-range plan to Ike. At first, he was dismayed by Eisenhower's lack of interest in II Corps, but Bradley refused to reveal his mounting frustration. Instead, he patiently built the case for including the unit in what Bradley called the final kill, arguing that it was tactically foolish not to make use of three experienced American divisions, that it was a grave error to give Anderson the II Corps' 9th Division (mixing nationalities and incompatible supply lines had wreaked havoc in prior operations), and that positive combat experience was absolutely necessary for soldiers who would soon be fighting in Europe. To Bradley's immense relief, Ike agreed, and the II Corps deputy presented his plan for II Corps to shift to the north of Anderson's First Army and make a wholly independent attack on the Axis stronghold of Bizerte.

Having sold Ike on giving II Corps a share of the North African victory by allowing it to capture Bizerte, Bradley would next have to persuade Alexander. In the meantime, however, II Corps was called on to assist Montgomery in breaking through the strong Axis defensive position known as the Mareth Line on March 26. That breakthrough was followed by a bloody slog as the Afrika Korps made a fighting retreat to another defensive position, the Chott Line, closer to the Tunisian coast. Frustrated with Montgomery, Alexander also continued to be unimpressed by II Corps, which, though it had assisted in the breakthrough, fought no truly decisive action. British high command freely leaked criticism of the Americans to the press, to the detriment not only of relations between the Allies but also between Patton and Bradley on the one hand and Ike on the other. To both II Corps leaders Eisenhower seemed unreasonably pro-British.

Despite the carping, Montgomery called on II Corps to help in his assault on the Chott Line. Patton responded by ordering the 9th Division together with the Big Red One to open the way for Ward's 1st Armored Division to drive against the Axis at the Chott Line. All Monty wanted was a harassing attack that would assist him, but Patton saw an opportunity either to divide the Axis line, thereby laying bare the enemy's vulnerable flanks, or even to drive the Axis forces lock, stock, and barrel into the sea. He rode out to Maknassy to warn Ward that if his division again failed to make progress he would relieve him. With that, Patton put the actual armored assault under the command of a World War I comrade, Clarence C. Benson, and designated the spearhead unit as "Benson Force."

Launched with much anticipation, Benson Force was almost instantly arrested by enemy resistance, whereupon Alexander suggested to Eisenhower that he fire Ward. Ike told Alexander to speak to Patton, who had already decided to relieve Ward himself—or, rather, to send his deputy commander, Bradley, to do the job for him. Orlando Ward was a close friend, and Bradley believed he was the victim of the weather and bad luck rather than inability, but he also knew that a soldier needed luck, and if he didn't have it, he was out—through no fault of his own. He delivered Patton's message.

Even with the 1st Armored Division under new command, Benson Force never succeeded in disrupting the Chott Line, although it did ceremonially link up with Montgomery's Eighth Army, thereby giving the impression that something had been accomplished. In the meantime, more through attrition than anything else, the Chott Line dissolved, and the Axis forces fell back again, to Enfidaville, farther north and closer to the coast. By this time, Bradley also received Alexander's approval for his Bizerte assault, and, on April 15, he officially assumed command of II Corps, freeing Patton to resume planning Operation Husky.

On taking his leave, Patton was generous in his praise of Bradley, telling him that he "never enjoyed service with anyone as much as you and trust that some day we can complete our warlike operations." As for Bradley, he at last assumed corps command, in the middle of a hot campaign, feeling that, thanks in no small measure to Patton, he had grown greatly on the job. Although he had "learned much, in terms of men and machines, about what was possible and not possible on the battlefield," Bradley felt that the most valuable lessons came from his close "observation of the personal interplay between the generals and their often conflicting views on strategy and tactics."[16] It was an interplay into which Omar Bradley would fully enter soon enough, after finishing the job in North Africa and taking II Corps to Sicily.

CHAPTER 8

II Corps Command

Omar Bradley had been sent to the war zone in a time of crisis, but when he assumed command of II Corps on April 16, 1943, Allied victory in the culminating battle to take Tunisia was practically a foregone conclusion. By the time Bradley took over II Corps, the Allies knew that Erwin Rommel was gone and that Jürgen von Arnim had taken over Afrika Korps and the other Axis units. Arnim was a capable commander, but his name and his presence lacked the Rommel magic. To defeat the Desert Fox, whom legend had portrayed as invincible, would have been a tremendous psychological triumph, one now denied the Allies.

Not that Arnim was in an enviable position. He had under his command perhaps a quarter-million troops, but he no longer controlled the air, he possessed fewer than one hundred battle-worthy tanks, and he was running low on all supplies, including food and ammunition. In stark contrast, the Allies now mustered 300 thousand men—20 divisions—with 1,400 tanks and an equal number of artillery assets. The

Allies enjoyed air supremacy, and their logistics systems were working smoothly. Supplies were ample. The Anglo-American forces were in an ideal position from which to administer the coup de grace to the Axis in Africa. Yet despite his many advantages, Deputy Allied Commander Harold Alexander persisted in applying the cautious "squeeze" strategy, using all available forces to close in on an enemy who had become contacted into a one hundred-mile perimeter. Slowly, methodically, he intended to push the foe up against the Tunisian coast. The First British Army, under Sir Kenneth Arthur Anderson, would make the major thrust, with Bernard Law Montgomery's Eighth British Army in a supporting role, acting against enemy positions at Enfidaville—with no one taking undue risks. The French XIX Corps would operate between the First and Eighth Armies to exploit offensive opportunities as they might arise, and the U.S. II Corps was relegated to covering Anderson's left (northern) flank. Instead of being assigned to capture Bizerte in an independent operation—as Bradley had planned and as both Eisenhower and Alexander had approved—II Corps was now expected only to assist First Army in taking this key stronghold.

Had George S. Patton Jr. still commanded II Corps, he almost certainly would have protested the final plan—and loudly. Bradley, however, actually liked the plan, if only because it assured II Corps a role in the final victory. Indeed, he was at the moment more comfortable in his relations with Alexander the Englishman than he was with Eisenhower the American. On April 16, he received what he characterized as a long and "patronizing" letter from Ike, offering what Bradley later characterized as "tactical suggestions which were dangerously ill-conceived and proof to me (if further proof were needed) that Ike had little grasp of sound battlefield tactics." Worse, Ike went on and on about the importance of American troops making a good showing. " 'As if I needed to be reminded of that!'" Bradley grumbled.[1] The new II Corps commander made it a point to file away the communiqué—unanswered.

Setting up II Corps headquarters on a hillside outside of the village of Bedia, Bradley introduced a regime he deemed far less flamboyant than Patton's. He aimed to lead with a more compassionate hand than his predecessor, coaxing rather than ordering, and always encouraging subordinates to solve problems through their own initiative.

The British component of the final Tunisian battle stepped off on the night of April 19th with an Eighth Army feint under Montgomery intended to fool Arnim into assuming that Eighth Army—not First Army—would make the main assault. The result, however, was a bloody rebuff for Montgomery, who had underestimated the ferocity of an enemy pushed to desperation. On April 22, the main assault, by Anderson's First Army, got under way. Both British corps involved in this action were stopped in their tracks by the Afrika Korps—again, despite all the disadvantages the Axis suffered.

In the meantime, on the 23rd, one day after Anderson began his attack, II Corps went into action. It faced east, toward Bizerte, and was arrayed along a broad forty-mile front between the First Army and the coast of the Mediterranean. Eisenhower's tactical directions were for Bradley to open his principal attack with armor along the Tine River Valley at the southern end of the II Corps sector. Having made extensive use of sand tables at Infantry School and West Point to study and understand terrain, Bradley looked closely at a landscape Ike had never seen for himself. As a result, he concluded that following Ike's directions would lead to disaster because the enemy held all the high ground, which he had thoroughly seeded with his antitank guns. Even though Ike's directions were tantamount to orders, Bradley believed that following them would end up in another Kasserine Pass, and he and his aides made it a point to derisively label the very route of advance Ike had specified "Mousetrap Valley."

Undemonstrative, ever cooperative, Omar Bradley was nevertheless by no means a man who simply followed orders. Instead, he advised his division commanders to stay off obvious routes, keep out of Mousetrap Valley, and make taking the high ground the number one priority. Only after the high ground had been captured would he bring up the tanks.

This was planning like an infantryman. Whereas an armor advocate, always looking for speed of movement, would make maximum use of the roads, Bradley was not afraid of a hard, foot-borne slog, provided it would sneak his men to a position from which they could dominate the topography of the battlefield. The recent lessons of blitzkrieg—lessons Bradley himself had eagerly absorbed on the eve of war—dictated Ike's tactics: leading off with tanks, following up with infantry. But Bradley saw that the terrain here was not the Polish plain or the Russian steppe.

Rugged and hilly, it did not lend itself to blitzkrieg. Deliberately, therefore, he reverted to what must have appeared to be the earlier mode of tactical thought, subordinating modern armor to old-fashioned foot soldiers. Although some contemporaries as well as later historians criticized Bradley as being overly cautious, no one ever accused him of inflexibility. Bradley adapted tactics to terrain and other circumstances, introducing into American military doctrine a suppleness that endures as a planning hallmark today.

A slog it was, methodical and met by resistance from what Bradley characterized as a fanatical enemy.

Fanatical? Fierce, perhaps, but methodical in its ferocity. Like Bradley, the Germans understood the importance of the terrain. They yielded the high ground grudgingly, exacting a high price from the attackers before retreating to the next available piece of high ground, sowing in their wake a deadly crop of land mines and pouring on the artillery.

Within the framework of the simple, broad orders Bradley issued, he allowed division commanders to work out for themselves the details of their assigned operations, but he always kept in close communication with them all, by phone first thing in the morning each morning, then face-to-face later in the day, every day. Bradley believed it essential for him to stay in contact with the terrain as his divisions advanced; besides, he wanted "to show the GI's that their commander was no rear-echelon tent hog."[2] It was an admirable practice that nevertheless nearly resulted in Bradley's being killed by artillery fire focused on a road junction.

Three days into the operation, on April 26, after advancing no more than five miles, II Corps ground to a halt, pinned down by fire from Hill 609, the commanding high ground of the entire sector. Now Bradley selected a play from the Patton playbook. He turned to Lieutenant Colonel Charles W. "Doc" Ryder, in command of the 34th Division, the most maligned unit of II Corps, and told him point-blank: "Get me that hill, and no one will ever again doubt the toughness of your division."[3]

Three attempts were repulsed, whereupon Bradley—in the best GI fashion—improvised, proposing to "Doc" Ryder that he use tanks as mobile artillery. No manual of armor doctrine and tactics sanctioned using tanks to assault a hill nearly 2 thousand feet in height, but Ryder heard his chief out and was more than game for a try.

In the meantime, orders reached Bradley from Anderson directing him to break off the assault on Hill 609, bypass it—in other words, leave the enemy in possession of the highest high ground in the area!—and then transfer one of his divisions to Anderson's First Army. Bradley refused both orders—the first, he later wrote, because it was "absurd" and the second because it violated the inter-Allied agreement that U.S. troops would remain under U.S. command. When he protested to Anderson, the British commander yielded on both counts, and by the morning of April 30, Ryder's infantry, supported by seventeen tanks, finally took Hill 609. German prisoners of war marveled at the unconventional use of armor, for which they had prepared no countermeasures. One "actually told us that the use of tanks had been unfair!"[4]

With the taking of Hill 609, the way was now clear for a full armored assault. As for Ryder's 34th Division, it emerged bloodied but emboldened, and went on to compile a superb combat record in the rest of the war.

⊢⇒══⇒⊣

Bradley's immediate tactical problems had been solved, but the fact remained that Anderson's First Army thrust, the crux of Alexander's squeeze strategy, had fizzled. Alexander took a new tack, sending the British IX Corps, augmented by other British units, on a narrow, focused drive toward Tunis. Bradley drew up new plans for II Corps to support this thrust, which was scheduled to step off on May 6. Taking Hill 609 had brought his corps to Mateur, a village beyond the hills. Poised now before flat land—perfect for armor—Bradley planned a two-pronged tank attack directed, in proven blitzkrieg fashion, against the enemy's rear, where it would have the greatest disruptive effect. It was a high-stakes gamble, which Ernest Harmon, commanding the 1st Armored Division, thought would cost as many as 50 tanks. But he agreed that the potential payoff was worth the risk. In the meantime, while Harmon thrust toward the enemy's rear, Bradley would deploy his three infantry divisions to support Anderson's First Army on its left flank while remaining in position to exploit any breakthrough Harmon might manage to make.

Tanks, infantry, close air support, pounding artillery, open ground—this was blitzkrieg, American style: a true combined arms action long before such tactics became an accepted feature of American military doctrine. The May 6 Anglo-American assault achieved the momentum that had been impossible with the earlier "squeeze" strategy. Harmon took his objectives, hitting the enemy in the rear and losing 47 tanks in the process, while the 3 II Corps infantry divisions took Chouigui (the main objective assigned in support of the First Army push) and closed in on Bizerte, which Major General Manton Eddy's 9th Division entered on May 7—unaided by the British. Two days later, Arnim surrendered, yielding as prisoners 150 thousand Italian and 100 thousand German soldiers. One of the pillars on which the myth of Axis invincibility rested, the Afrika Korps, was not only defeated, it no longer existed. Bradley sent Ike a cable, exultant as it was laconic: "Mission accomplished." For his part, Ike responded generously, advising the dean of American war correspondents, Ernie Pyle, to "go and discover Bradley."[5] It was the beginning of the low-profile Bradley's rise to national celebrity.

Any summary chronology of World War II ticks off the North African campaign as the Allies' first big victory against the Axis, followed by the invasion of Sicily, the second major victory. The view from the ground, however, was very different.

To begin with, the top American generals, George C. Marshall and Ike Eisenhower, never wanted to spend much time in the Mediterranean, which they considered a dangerous diversion from what should have been the main objective: an invasion of France across the English Channel. In contrast to his superiors, Bradley would come away from both the North African and Sicilian campaigns convinced that Winston Churchill and the British high command had been right to insist on undertaking these "peripheral" operations first. An attempt to invade France in 1943 would have been disastrously premature. Nevertheless, Bradley found very little to like about Operation Husky, the Allied plan for the invasion of Sicily.

Originally, two options had been drawn up. The first was the encirclement and isolation of German and Italian forces by means of a main amphibious assault in the Strait of Messina and Calabria combined with a secondary assault on Sicily itself. This, Bradley believed, was the logical approach, with potential to bag all Axis forces on Sicily. Yet, to Bradley's chagrin, the option was dismissed out of hand, due—as he saw it—to a failure of strategic vision among high command. The Casablanca Conference in January 1943 had been convened in part to decide the next step after the conquest of North Africa. The decision was to take Sicily, but the matter of where to go from there was left open. Since an assault on Calabria was an assault on mainland Italy, it was deemed beyond the scope of the Casablanca mandate, and so was simply given no further thought.

Omar Bradley is judged by many military historians an important tactician but a less considerable strategist. It is true that, like Patton, Bradley was not in a position to determine overall strategy until the end of the European campaign; however, whereas Patton repeatedly admitted that he had little interest in strategy—he believed that skillful tactics vigorously executed could redeem the worst strategy, but that the best strategy could never compensate for poor tactics—Bradley showed a keener and more critical grasp of strategy than he is generally given credit for. He was right to denounce as timid and unimaginative the assault option chosen by Allied high command. Operation Husky was little more than a blunt frontal assault on Sicily. It would result in the taking of that island—at significant cost—but, by failing to isolate and encircle the Axis defenders there, it would also allow many thousands to withdraw, in Dunkirk fashion, across the Strait of Messina and into Italy—an outcome that would help turn the Italian campaign into a bloody heartbreak spanning the entire duration of the European war.

As with operations in North Africa, overall command of the invasion was Eisenhower's responsibility, with operational command entrusted to Alexander, who headed the newly created Fifteenth Army Group, consisting of Montgomery's Eighth British Army and the U.S. I Armored Corps, commanded by Patton. The designation of Patton's unit would be changed to the Seventh U.S. Army as soon as it landed on Sicily. Allied planners refrained from calling it an army before that point in order to enhance Operation Mincemeat, an elaborate program of deceptions and decoys so successful that only two German divisions were on hand to oppose the landings when they were made on July 10, 1943.

The Fifteenth Army Group fielded a total of eight divisions, including airborne, commando, and Ranger units. Three of the divisions, the 45th Infantry (under Troy Middleton), the 1st Infantry (Terry de la Mesa Allen), and the 3rd Infantry (Lucian Truscott) were constituents of Bradley's II Corps, which operated as part of Patton's Seventh Army.

Beyond the initial critical misstep of rejecting the bold strategy of isolation and encirclement, the Allies subsequently fell to squabbling throughout the planning of the assault. Bradley faulted an absence of guidance from the top—by which he meant a deficiency of strong leadership from Eisenhower—for creating a plan he dismissed as "pure Leavenworth textbook."[6] It was a conventional pincer movement, in which Montgomery's Eighth British Army was to land in the southeast corner of Sicily, near Syracuse, while Patton's Seventh landed near Palermo, on the northwest coast. Supplied through the ports of Syracuse and Palermo, the two armies would advance along their respective coastlines to converge at Messina at the northeast tip of Sicily, just across the strait that separates the island from the Italian mainland.

The plan, Bradley felt, fell far short of what could be accomplished by a simultaneous assault on mainland Calabria and Sicily, but, conventional though it was, if the pincers movement could be executed quickly, it might well succeed in enveloping the island and cutting off the Axis avenue of mainland retreat. Understandably, however, none of the American commanders was passionately enthusiastic about the plan, and when Montgomery condemned it outright as "a dog's breakfast," a disastrous case of "penny-packet" warfare that imprudently divided the assault forces, spreading them out over some 600 miles of Sicilian coastline, no one jumped to its defense. Instead, Monty's objection triggered three months of wayward wrangling, among the British themselves and between the British and the Americans, culminating in an explosive meeting on April 29, 1943, which was followed three days later by a comical anticlimax that suddenly resolved the dispute.

On May 2, Montgomery walked into Allied headquarters, Algiers, and asked to see Walter Bedell "Beetle" Smith. Told that Ike's chief of staff was in the lavatory, Montgomery strode down the hall to the men's room, cornered Smith there, and took him to a mirror hanging over the sink. Just as depicted in the 1970 film *Patton*, Monty breathed on the mirror, then, using his finger, traced the inverted triangle of Sicily. He went on to trace out a plan in which his Eighth Army landed at two locations on the northeast corner of Sicily on either side of Messina while Patton's Seventh Army made three landings below Montgomery, along the eastern coast of the island, at Gela, Scoglitti, and Licata. The sole purpose of these American landings would be to support Montgomery's principal assault on Messina. There would be no Anglo-American pincer and no division of forces. Instead, the American army would do what Montgomery always wanted the American army to do: play second fiddle to him.

Patton was outraged, but figured he could somehow find a more active role once the operation was actually under way. Bradley, however, was stunned. First, the Allies had rejected a superb plan, then they managed to transform a mediocre plan into a downright bad plan. That the final plan emerged from an Algerian toilet must have seemed fitting to Bradley, but he was determined to make the best of it.

<hr>

Bradley was worried about more than having to execute a bad plan. A plan, good or bad, was one thing, but a soldier, the individual GI, was the army, and Bradley had observed two serious weaknesses in the men of II Corps during their drive to Bizerte: an unwillingness to reconnoiter, to maintain contact with the enemy, and to close with him; and a distressing tendency to surrender when outnumbered. The first defect he attributed to a lack of aggressiveness among the junior officers of the corps. The second he believed was the result of unrealistic training back in the States. In a message to General Marshall, Bradley pointed out that, in stateside war games:

> [W]hen two forces meet, the umpires invariably decide that the smaller force must withdraw, or if greatly outnumbered, it must surrender. . . . No means are provided for giving proportionate weight to the many intangibles of warfare, such as morale, training, leadership, conditioning. . . . I believe that very few circumstances arise where surrender is actually justified. A greatly

outnumbered force can accomplish wonders by vigorous and aggressive action.[7]

This concern about the fighting spirit of the individual soldier was typical of Bradley the leader of men. He determined that both the commander and deputy commander of 1st Division, Terry de la Mesa Allen and Theodore Roosevelt Jr., would have to be relieved as soon as circumstances permitted. Brave and aggressive, they were nonetheless clearly incapable of instilling and maintaining effective discipline in their subordinate officers and men.

+⚔+

Operation Husky was launched before dawn on July 10, 1943. At that time, it was biggest Allied operation of the war—it would be eclipsed only by the Normandy landings of June 6, 1944—and involved 180 thousand U.S. and British troops, 2,590 ships, and thousands of aircraft—although the airborne operations—paratroop and glider assaults—that preceded the principal landings were blown far off course by unfavorable winds and so, without these initial assaults, Axis resistance was stiffer than it would otherwise have been. Worse, sandbars grounded many landing craft, and, in 1st Division's landing sector, the sand was so soft that Allen was unable to get his artillery and tanks ashore. Middleton's division had some similar problems. Nevertheless, Operation Mincemeat had worked so well that German strength in the landing zone was, on balance, relatively weak. Moreover, the men displayed far more aggressiveness than Bradley had good reason to expect of them.

While Bradley's II Corps divisions landed on the southwest coast— the 3rd Infantry at Licata, the 1st at Gela, and the 45th Infantry Division at Scoglitti and points south of it—Montgomery's two British Eighth Army corps, the X and XIII, landed between Pozallo and Syracuse on the east coast. The British met with virtually no opposition, XIII Corps taking Syracuse on the very day that it landed. German armor heavily counterattacked the Big Red One at Gela on July 11, however, whereupon American warships riding offshore unleashed an intensive artillery bombardment that saved 1st Division and the American landings generally.

The action instilled in Bradley intense respect for the navy and great satisfaction in the coordination between the naval and ground components of the assault.

With Patton, however, Bradley worked less smoothly. During the course of July 11, Bradley ordered one of his units to hold fast until a threatening pocket of Germans had been cleared out. Patton, seeing only that a 1st Division unit was apparently stalled, went over Bradley's head, ordering Allen not to hold, but to attack. The result was that the unit in question was temporarily cut off. Enraged, Bradley complained to Patton, who humbly apologized—but who later complained to Eisenhower that the II Corps commander was insufficiently aggressive. An infuriated Bradley was now convinced that Patton did not know the difference between aggressiveness and recklessness. As it turned out, Ike was about to draw the same conclusion. When he visited Patton's command post on July 12, the Seventh Army commander boasted of his actions on the front, how he had deliberately and extensively exposed himself to fire in order to inspire his men to victory. Bradley thought that this meeting and these boasts marked a turning point of historical importance, Ike's loss of faith in Patton. Ike, Bradley believed, now came to see Patton as too reckless for command above that of a field army. The change in attitude likely thrust Bradley ahead of Patton as a candidate for army group command once the European invasion began.

⊬━━⊹

By July 12, the Anglo-American forces were firmly established on shore, but it was at this point, Bradley observed, that the fog of an ill-conceived plan became thickest. At least Bradley and Patton were on the same page, both assuming that Montgomery would push up the east coast through Catania to Messina—thereby blocking an Axis withdrawal to Calabria—while the Seventh Army advanced due north from its beachheads through Enna and Nicosia to the north coast road, on which it would make a sharp turn east to descend upon Messina, catching the rest of the Axis forces between itself and the British Eighth Army.

As it turned out, Monty had other plans. All of his forces except for XXX Corps, under Oliver Leese, were blocked before Catania. Monty ordered Leese to advance around the west face of Mount Etna in order to swing northeast toward Messina, thereby breaking through the Axis forces blocking the coast highway. This done, the pincer snapping shut on Messina would be exclusively British, consisting of XXX Corps and the rest of Monty's Eighth Army. The Seventh U.S. Army would yet again be relegated to protecting the rear and left flank of the Eighth British. Montgomery discussed the plan with no one, but high-handedly ordered Leese into action on July 13, demanding—after the fact—that Alexander order Patton to halt his advance and make way for Leese's approach.

To Bradley's stunned consternation, Patton made no protest. Perhaps, Bradley guessed, the Seventh Army commander sensed Eisenhower's growing distrust of him and was loath to provide him with any possible excuse for relieving him of command. Now II Corps had to give up much of what it had gained, including possession of the northerly route to Messina, and generally rein in the momentum of attack. Bradley's G–2, Benjamin A. "Monk" Dickson, wrote later: "General Bradley executed this preposterous order silently and skillfully, but inwardly he was as hot as Mount Etna."[8] He had been poised to break out, to run—fast—to the north coast and thence to Messina. This would have had the effect of easing the pressure on Montgomery at Catania, allowing him to resume his drive to Messina as well. The Anglo-American pincers would have been faster, bigger, and more crushing than the exclusively British operation Monty now envisaged. As Bradley saw it, the Allies were sacrificing an opportunity to cut off completely the Axis retreat to the mainland.

Although Patton had not confronted Alexander over Montgomery's usurpation of the assault on Messina, he was not content to merely to support the Eighth British Army. On July 15, 1943, he formed a provisional corps under Lieutenant General Geoffrey Keyes to advance on Palermo. Bradley regarded Palermo as an objective of no concrete strategic significance, but he did admit that possession of Sicily's biggest and most famous city was of psychological value. The objective fell to Keyes on July 22.

In the meantime, by July 17, German forces had set up the first of three lines of defense, which extended from south of Catania across to

San Stefano on the north coast. The defenders occupied mountainous terrain that greatly aided them by inhibiting armored advance, and the high-handed Montgomery soon bogged down. He would not break through to Catania until August 5.

While the fight for Sicily pounded on, back in Rome Benito Mussolini was deposed, removed from power on July 25 by the very Fascist Council he had created. This shook Adolf Hitler sufficiently for him to authorize preparations to evacuate German forces from Sicily—an eventuality that Albert Kesselring, commander of Axis forces on this front, had already envisioned. The Germans began a fighting withdrawal from their first defensive line on July 27, continuing, as they fought, the skillful exploitation of the Sicilian terrain to slow Allied progress and to make the Allied advance costly.

Allen launched a reckless assault against the German position at Troina and was thrown back because he had badly underestimated German strength there. The Big Red One fought a vicious battle, which stretched over an entire week. Concluding that Allen was fighting valiantly but utterly without discipline, Bradley personally took over tactical planning of the battle. After the Germans finally withdrew, he acted on his earlier judgment concerning both Allen and Roosevelt and relieved them, respectively, as commander and deputy commander of the Big Red One.

The fall of Troina was followed by the Germans' defeat at their fallback position, Adrano. That greatly accelerated Kesselring's efforts to get his forces off Sicily, and, on the night of August 11th, he began the evacuation, ultimately saving 40 thousand German and 70 thousand Italian troops to fight another day—on the mainland. With them went some 10 thousand vehicles and about 17 thousand tons of supplies. Belatedly, both Montgomery and Patton launched amphibious assaults in a hopeless effort to cut off the retreat.

+⊨⊨+

Allied victory in Sicily was assured, but had been diminished by the Axis withdrawal. Patton, who had failed to protest Montgomery's foolish and humiliating revision of the plan to assault Messina, now felt the pressure.

Personally, that pressure may have manifested itself in the two infamous "slapping incidents" that nearly ended Patton's military career. On August 3, during the battle for Troina, he condemned as a coward, verbally abused, and slapped a soldier, Private Charles H. Kuhl, who was in an evacuation hospital suffering from battle fatigue and (unknown to Patton) dysentery and malaria. On August 10, in another field hospital, Patton accused a second soldier of cowardice. He not only slapped Private Paul G. Bennett, but pointed his trademark ivory-handled revolver at him, threatening to shoot him because, so said Patton, he was a "yellow son of a bitch."[9]

Strategically, the pressure kindled in Patton a burning desire to beat Montgomery to Messina. Without doubt, Messina was Sicily's strategic prize, and Monty's bid to deny the American army a piece of it was faltering. However, by the time Patton began his race for Messina, Kesselring had already evacuated the bulk of his forces to the mainland. For this reason, Bradley believed Patton's determination to beat Monty to Messina was nearly irrational. The horses were already out of the barn; no need to break your neck closing the door. Bradley ordered the Big Red One, now commanded by Clarence R. Huebner, to fight alongside the 9th Division under Eddy in an advance on Messina. In the meantime, Lucian Truscott's 3rd Division was bearing down on Messina along the north road. To accelerate the advance, Patton ordered a regimental combat team from Troy Middleton's 45th Division to make a hazardous amphibious assault by way of an end run against the town. With Truscott in tow, Bradley protested the order to Patton, pointing out that the advance of 3rd Division was now so rapid that there was a distinct possibility that Middleton and Truscott would collide outside of Messina in a nightmare of friendly fire. Patton responded by testily reiterating the order.

As it turned out, on the night of August 15, Middleton's combat team did land squarely among Truscott's troops. The commanders had prepared for this eventuality, however, and narrowly avoided catastrophe. For his part, Truscott generously invited one of Middleton's battalion's to accompany his men into Messina.

As commander of II Corps, to which Truscott's 3rd Division and Middleton's 45th belonged, the capture of Messina, the culminating battle in the 38-day-long conquest of Sicily, was Omar Bradley's victory. It was distinctly bittersweet. When the city's civilian officials tried to surrender to Truscott, he declined in deference to Patton's orders that only the commander of Seventh Army was authorized to accept the surrender of the city. Bradley had to order the bulk of Truscott's men to hold their positions in the hills surrounding Messina until Patton's arrival, so that he could enter the city at the head of an armed cavalcade. In the meantime, Truscott and his men watched as the last of the German and Italian forces in and around Messina made their way across the strait to Calabria.

Bradley was so enraged by what he considered Patton's megalomania that he was tempted to upstage Patton by entering the city before him and then greeting the Seventh Army commander when he arrived. But, as always, he restrained himself, and joined Patton at 10 o'clock in the morning on August 17, when he led a motorcade into Messina, officially accepted the city's surrender, then greeted a British officer who arrived an hour later. Shaking Patton's hand, the officer remarked, "It was a jolly good race. I congratulate you."[10]

The commanding general of II Corps was not amused. The Anglo-American invasion force had lost 5,532 killed, 14,410 wounded, and 2,869 missing. At the time, everyone—Bradley included—assumed that they had killed a great many German and Italian troops. In fact, only a few thousand had died and many more had been allowed to cross the Messina Strait. The Anglo-American victory was important yet also hollow.

Bradley (pointing) with Lieutenant General Lesley J. McNair during Third Army maneuvers in Louisiana, 1941. (National Archives and Records Administration)

The "GI General" closely observes Privates First Class A. J. Thomas of Bradshaw, Maryland, and Peter R. Saratto of Marion, Connecticut, firing a small mortar during pre-D-Day training at Swyre, England, in April 1944. (Signal Corps photo, National Archives and Records Administration)

(left) *Lieutenant General Omar N. Bradley, January 24, 1944. (Truman Presidential Museum and Library)*

(below) *In this undated photograph, Bradley decorates his Third Army commander, George S. Patton Jr. (Signal Corps photo, National Archives and Records Administration)*

(top) *Twelfth Army Group commander Bradley visits with First Army commander Courtney Hodges in January 1945, at the end of the Battle of the Bulge. (Signal Corps photo, National Archives and Records Administration)*

(bottom) *In March 1945, Ike and Bradley, with Courtney Hodges and III Corps commander Major General James Van Fleet (partially hidden behind Bradley's helmet), cross—for the first time—the Rhine River at Remagen. (Signal Corps photo, National Archives and Records Administration)*

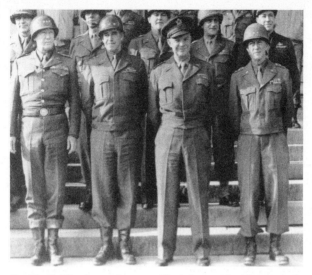

Dwight D. Eisenhower, Supreme Allied Commander, Europe, with Third Army commander George S. Patton Jr., Twelfth U.S. Army Group commander Bradley, and First Army commander Courtney Hodges. (National Archives and Records Administration)

Eisenhower, Bradley, and others look in disbelief at the charred bodies of prisoners burned in a concentration camp at Gotha, Germany. Patton stands to the far right. A helmeted Bradley is next to Eisenhower. (Truman Presidential Museum and Library)

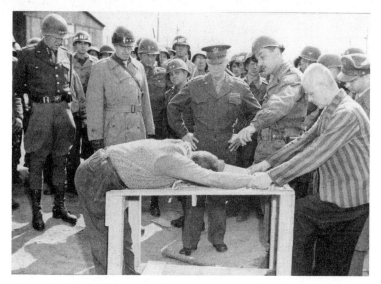

Patton, Bradley, and Eisenhower (left to right) observe as newly liberated concentration camp inmates demonstrate a Nazi torture technique. (Truman Presidential Museum and Library)

Truman takes the presidential salute in Berlin, July 1945. Eisenhower and Patton stand to the president's right. Secretary of War Henry Stimson (partially obscured by the microphone) and Bradley stand to Truman's left. (Truman Presidential Museum and Library)

President Truman poses with Eisenhower, Patton, and Bradley at the Potsdam Conference, outside of Berlin, July 20, 1945. (Truman Presidential Museum and Library)

Ike Eisenhower swears in Omar Bradley, his successor as U.S. Army chief of staff, February 7, 1948. President Truman and Secretary of the Army Kenneth C. Royall look on. (Truman Presidential Museum and Library)

(below) *General of the Army Omar Nelson Bradley, 1950. (Truman Presidential Museum and Library)*

(above) *General Hoyt S. Vandenberg, the second chief of staff of the newly independent U.S. Air Force (left), poses with Chief of Naval Operations Admiral Louis E. Denfield and U.S. Army Chief of Staff Omar Bradley in 1948. When Bradley became the nation's first chairman of the Joint Chiefs of Staff the following year, he took on the difficult task of mediating between the demands of the air force and those of the navy for the lion's share of defense funds. (Truman Presidential Museum and Library)*

Omar Bradley, chair of NATO's military committee and its inner circle "standing group," addresses standing group members in 1950. (Truman Presidential Museum and Library)

President Truman, returned from his Wake Island meeting with MacArthur, poses with his advisers. Secretary of State Dean Acheson stands to the president's left, and Secretary of Defense George C. Marshall to his right. Chairman of the Joint Chiefs of Staff Bradley is at the far right of the photograph. (Truman Presidential Museum and Library)

CHAPTER 9

D-Day

No one in the British or American armies had a more profound sense of history than George S. Patton Jr. He saw himself as the latest in a long line of conquerors of Sicily, stretching back nearly to the beginnings of recorded history. There was justification in this view. After all, it was he, not Bernard Law Montgomery, who had reached Messina first—and Messina was considered the strategic jewel of Sicily ever since the Carthaginians first sacked it in 396 B.C. Yet no general of ancient Carthage ever had to worry about the repercussions of slapping a pair of enlisted soldiers. As they became increasingly known to the public, the "slapping incidents" robbed Patton of much of the Sicilian glory he had earned and to which he believed himself entitled. As for Montgomery, his having come in second at Messina disqualified him—temporarily at least—for the glory of conquest as well. From the American point of view, Patton's fall from grace and Montgomery's runner-up showing left Omar Bradley in the best light of all the major commanders of the Sicily campaign. To be sure, he lacked the Pattonesque swagger that befit a conqueror, but, thanks in part to the publicity provided by Ernie Pyle, he had more than enough of the air of democratic hero about him to figure in the public imagination—if not as Sicily's fire-breathing conqueror, then at least as its benign liberator.

Not that this new identity was entirely a matter of public relations. In a strictly military sense, Bradley and II Corps had done most of the heavy lifting that resulted in the taking of Messina. Saddled with a bad plan—so bad that it was barely a plan at all—Bradley had improvised his way to a position from which Patton, much against Bradley's own better judgment, could order him to beat Montgomery to Messina and end the Sicilian campaign on a note of distinctly American triumph.

Generals George C. Marshall and Dwight D. Eisenhower hoped that the victories in North Africa and Sicily, however imperfect, had finally cleared the way for what they, in contrast to their British colleagues, considered the main event: the cross-Channel invasion of the European continent. There was agreement between Franklin D. Roosevelt and Winston Churchill that this operation—originally code named Roundup, and now called Overlord—would take place in May 1944, but Churchill persisted in advocating a program of peripheral strikes to precede Overlord, including actions in Greece, the Balkans, Norway, and Italy. In the end, at the so-called Quadrant conference held in Quebec in August 1943, Churchill, Roosevelt, and the Combined Chiefs (military representatives from the U.S. and Britain) decided on dividing the ongoing military effort in Europe between Overlord and a full invasion of mainland Italy.

Although the Quadrant Conference gave Churchill a big piece of what he wanted—a continuation of his much-cherished approach to Germany via the "soft underbelly" of Europe—it also resulted in the decision that an American general, not a British one, would lead Operation Overlord as well as the European campaign that would follow. The Quadrant Conference ended with everyone assuming that Marshall would be that American commander. As for operations in Italy, they would be commanded by Harold Alexander and would consist of a dual attack, beginning with Montgomery's Eighth British Army against Calabria and followed days later by the Fifth Army, which would land at Salerno, south of Naples, in coordination with other British landings at Taranto.

Fifth Army was commanded by Mark Clark, the tall, handsome general that Churchill called an 'American eagle.' Eisenhower tapped Omar Bradley as Clark's understudy, to assume Fifth Army command should anything happen to Clark. Thus, once again, Bradley found himself subordinated to an officer whose approach to command differed sharply from his own and about whom he had serious misgivings. Bradley admired Clark's valor—a battalion commander in World War I, he had been wounded in action—but he believed that Clark lacked sufficient experience with large forces to be thrust into combat command of an entire army. More seriously, Bradley was disturbed by Clark's personality, which, in his opinion, came perilously close to that of Patton: he was too hungry for glory and personal advancement. Ironically perhaps, Bradley pointed out that Patton likewise distrusted Clark, judging him "too damned slick" and far more interested in "bettering his own future than winning the war."[1]

Was Bradley envious? Did *he* want Fifth Army command? Could his doubts have been just so much sour grapes?

Perhaps, but it isn't likely. Bradley's misgivings about Clark were almost certainly sincere, as was his skepticism concerning the composition of Fifth Army, which consisted of an American corps and a British one, despite the fact that the Allies had never experienced much success mixing British and American units in the same army. Moreover, as it turned out, Bradley had very little time to envy Clark. Marshall moved headlong with Overlord and decided that it was of utmost importance to establish an American army headquarters in Britain immediately. He cabled Eisenhower on August 25 nominating Bradley for the job and asking Ike to release him for it. Eisenhower responded to Marshall with high praise for Bradley, yet initially pushed Clark for the job of First Army creator and commander. Eisenhower's message to Marshall, August 27, 1943, is most telling: "Bradley is a standout in any position and is running absolutely true to form." By the conclusion of the North African campaign, Patton, Clark, and Bradley had each received promotion to temporary lieutenant general, and Ike told Marshall that any of them would meet his needs, although he allowed that, of "the three, Bradley is the best rounded in all respects, counting experience, and he has the great characteristic of never giving his commander one moment of worry." The same, of course, could not be said of the volatile Patton, whom Ike characterized as his preeminent combat commander, never affected by a tendency to yield to caution, fatigue or doubt and never allowing his troops to be affected by these. Nevertheless, in contrast to the "rounded" Bradley, Patton (Ike judged) was "a one sided individual . . . apt at times to display exceedingly poor judgment and unjustified temper." As for Clark, Eisenhower deemed him "the ablest and most experienced officer . . . in planning of amphibious operations," which Ike knew were key to Overlord. "As you can see," Eisenhower admitted to Marshall, "I personally am distressed at the thought of losing Bradley because I have come to lean on him so heavily in absorbing part of the burdens that otherwise fall directly upon me. . . . This very reason probably makes him your obvious choice [for First Army commander], but if you should take Clark, I could shove Bradley immediately into command of Fifth Army. . . ."[2]

To Eisenhower's great credit, he sent Marshall a new cable the very next day: "I have been thinking over what I told you in my telegram of the other day reference Bradley and other commanders. The truth of the matter is that you should take Bradley and, moreover, I will make him available on any date you say. I will get along."[3]

Marshall replied on September 1, asking Eisenhower to tell Bradley to prepare to leave for England to head an *army* headquarters and probably also to develop an *army group* headquarters. But Ike said nothing to Bradley until September 3, when Bradley flew to Alexander's command post at Cassibile, Sicily, where Eisenhower, who had just accepted Italy's surrender, greeted Bradley with the "good news" that he had just been given "a fancy new job." Bradley sat silently as Eisenhower passed on Marshall's assignment. "I could not have been more stunned or elated," Bradley wrote later. He well understood that his new assignment was "going to grow into the most important combat job in the U.S. Army in World War II. No soldier could have wished for more."[4]

⊬═══⊬

If Bradley had harbored any envy of Clark before receiving his new assignment, he now felt only elation mixed with relief that he would not be involved in Italy after all. Ever the realist, Bradley foresaw a long and costly campaign in Italy with uncertain results.

Bradley bade farewell to II Corps on September 8—his troops lining the road to the airfield, presenting arms, dipping guidons, and otherwise saluting as his car passed—and set off for England. At the London airport, Lieutenant General Jacob L. Devers, commanding general of the European Theater of Operations (ETO), greeted him.

Bradley had an urgent fear that Devers might be appointed Overlord army group commander, with Courtney Hodges and himself leading armies under him. To Bradley, as well as Ike (who dismissed him as a ".22 caliber" man[5]), Jake Devers was a lightweight. There was, however, little time to worry about Devers, as, after a single week in England, Bradley flew to Washington to choose key personnel for his First Army. General Marshall was too busy to met with Bradley at the Pentagon, but he invited him along on a flight to Omaha, Nebraska, where Marshall was to address an American Legion convention. En route, Bradley made characteristically good use of the time to review with Marshall in detail the Sicily campaign, putting the emphasis on lessons learned. Patton, effectively suspended from the war as a result of the slapping incidents, had asked Bradley to put in a good word for him. But Bradley said nothing to Marshall about Patton.

On his return to Washington, Bradley was summoned to the White House to brief the president on Sicily and to give FDR an opportunity to speak to the man who was now one of his top commanders. Unexpectedly, Roosevelt in turn briefed Bradley on the biggest and most secret undertaking of the entire war: the Manhattan Project. On one level, this was a terrible breach of security on the president's part. After all, a ground commander in Europe was by no means officially in a "need-to-know" position with regard to the atomic bomb. For his part, Bradley was flabbergasted by what he heard, but he had sufficient presence of mind to mention the conversation to no one. Why had Roosevelt made so free with the information? Bradley believed that the president was worried that the Germans might have the bomb by the time of the Allied invasion. With all the imponderables attendant on Operation Overlord, one can only imagine what place this talk of an all-annihilating super weapon—perhaps already in German hands—occupied in Bradley's mind.

Of more immediate concern was the selection of key personnel for Operation Overlord. By this time, Bradley had learned that he would not only command First Army, but also First U.S. Army Group—at least until final decisions had been made concerning just who would lead Overlord. He had the heavy responsibility of staffing both commands at a time when good men were in very heavy demand and good men with combat experience were virtually impossible to come by.

Bradley raided his key II Corps staff for the top First Army staff positions, then added Joseph J. "Red" O'Hare to serve as G–1, his personnel chief. O'Hare was a vintage Bradley hire. He was a friend as well as a West Point football teammate. His personal attributes did not make for a conventionally impressive resume: "thoroughly unpopular, imperious and autocratic, capricious in his judgments, and not too bright." But Bradley *knew* him and had *played* with him. These experiences convinced Bradley that O'Hare had "a lot of common sense. . . . His mule-headedness would serve us well in France and Germany."[6]

While Bradley could choose his staff, he had no control over the ultimate choice of Overlord command. He was pulling for Marshall, but the choice went to Eisenhower. Bradley confessed to mixed feelings about this, but consoled himself that Marshall would still be chief of staff in Washington.

+>==<+

Shortly after Ike's arrival in London on January 15, 1944, Overlord command quickly took shape. Despite the setbacks he had suffered in Sicily, Montgomery had assumed legendary status in Britain and even in America. He, not Harold Alexander (whom Bradley believed was much more capable), was appointed by Churchill and Field Marshall Sir Alan Brooke as deputy Overlord commander—leading all ground forces in the Normandy landings as Ike's immediate subordinate. It was agreed that, once the landings had been completed and a lodgment achieved, Monty would assume command of all British forces as head of the Twenty-first Army Group, simultaneously relinquishing overall ground command to the American commander of the First U.S. Army Group. Bradley held that post at present, but the appointment, he understood, was an interim position, his only until a permanent commander was named. Finally, following the initial breakout inland from the lodgments, the position of ground commander would cease to exist, and Eisenhower would assume direct control of the ground campaign.

The naval component of Operation Overlord was commanded by Royal Navy admiral Bertram H. Ramsay, an appointment that greatly pleased Eisenhower. Command of the air component was more complex, with Eisenhower and two British officers, Arthur Tedder and Arthur "Bomber" Harris, each playing somewhat overlapping roles.

For a short time, the issue of who would assume permanent command of the First U.S. Army Group was in doubt. Eisenhower wanted no one other than the present holder of that position, Bradley, but Marshall suggested Hodges, and, of course, Patton's name also loomed prominently. Ike also had to consider Lesley McNair and Fourth U.S. Army chief William H. "Big Simp" Simpson. Hodges and Simpson he eliminated because they lacked large-unit combat command experience. McNair, whom Eisenhower revered, was almost totally deaf—a disability Ike believed disqualified him from high operational command. Patton, as far as Ike was concerned, had shown himself unfit for anything higher than an army command. This therefore left Ike's original choice; he cabled Marshall accordingly, and Marshall approved Bradley's permanent appointment.

By the time Bradley's appointment was officially announced, Patton was in England, but still in professional limbo. Instead of assigning him command of an army, Bradley and Eisenhower chose to exploit his notoriety—they knew, in particular, that the Germans considered him the best of the Allied field commanders—by making him "commander" of a fictitious army in a program of deception even more ambitious than Operation Mincemeat had been. Called Operation Fortitude, the deception campaign combined wooden dummy aircraft and inflatable faux tanks as well as other decoys (many designed and fabricated by stagecraft experts from Hollywood and the British film industry) with phony radio traffic that was intended to be intercepted and disinformation supplied to German intelligence via a network of double agents, all designed to dupe the enemy into thinking that the cross-Channel invasion would land at what was indeed the most logical spot on the French coast, the Pas de Calais, rather than at Normandy.

Even as Bradley greeted the decoy general, he knew that Eisenhower intended ultimately to put him into the action for real. Patton was, after all, too brilliant to waste. Yet Bradley was uncomfortable and dissatisfied. Late in life he admitted that, had it been left to him, he would not have included Patton in Overlord at all. In part, he had doubts about Patton's willingness to take orders from him, his former subordinate; but, even more important, Bradley was convinced that Patton had demonstrated in Sicily that he did not know how to command an army.

Bradley's attitude toward Patton would evolve and change profoundly during the breakout phase of the Normandy invasion and beyond, but, for now, he was by no means pleased to have Patton in his command, and when two new incidents threatened to bring about Patton's relief before Overlord was launched, Bradley encouraged Ike to fire him. The first incident was a rumor that Patton had encouraged soldiers to shoot rather than take into custody surrendering enemy troops during the Sicily campaign. Even as this potentially destructive rumor duly faded, Patton stirred new controversy with an impromptu speech he made on April 25 to a group of British ladies who had created a "Welcome Club" for American GIs stationed near their little Cheshire town of Knutsford. As Patton recalled it, he had remarked that the Welcome Club was a wonderful idea because it was "the evident destiny of the British and Americans, and, of course, the Russians, to rule the world, [and] the better we know each other, the better job we will do."[7] But the press reported the remark conspicuously without the mention of the Russians and claimed that this omission was Patton's calculated and spectacular insult to the gallant Soviet ally.

Coming after so many other Patton gaffes, the Knutsford incident was the proverbial last straw, and Eisenhower cabled Marshall his intention to relieve the offending general and send him back to the States. Bradley unreservedly concurred with Ike's decision, and he agreed with his selection of Hodges to command Third U.S. Army, which was being created for Patton. Patton, however, was reprieved; after a personal meeting with Ike, he managed to retain command by the skin of his teeth.

The extent to which Bradley at this stage of his career distrusted Patton may be gauged not just by his willingness to see a brilliant combat commander sacrificed, but also to condone his replacement by Courtney Hodges, an officer about whom Bradley himself expressed serious reservations. Hodges had been appointed Bradley's own First Army deputy commander and was then was moved up to First Army command when Bradley was named to permanent command of First Army Group. Bradley had always liked him, but now that Hodges reported directly to him, he worried that he was indecisive and overly conservative.

About the last addition to First Army Group, a newly created Ninth Army under William "Big Simp" Simpson, Bradley harbored no doubts. Simpson was the kind of simple, straightforward, methodical, but aggressive commander he best understood and most liked.

Problems of personnel persisted as Bradley turned to the details of implementing the Overlord plan. He was never one of the principal Overlord planners, and—especially early on—he had limited scope within which to adjust it. The plan allocated to his First Army three corps for the assault on Normandy. The V Corps was to be commanded by Leonard T. "Gee" Gerow, an old friend who had seen action in the Punitive Expedition against Pancho Villa and in World War I. The other two commanders, Roscoe B. Woodruff (VII Corps) and Willis D. Crittenberger (XIX Corps) were unknown quantities to Bradley, even though Woodruff was both a West Point classmate and a fraternity brother. Despite his high opinion of Gerow as an outstanding soldier, Bradley knew that he, like Woodruff, lacked combat experience in command of a large force. The same was true of Crittenberger, but his status soon became a moot point because he was transferred to Italy.

Gerow's V Corps and Woodruff's VII Corps were slated to spearhead the D-Day landings, with XIX Corps held as a floating reserve to follow up. The man Bradley really wanted to lead at least one of the spearhead corps was Lucian Truscott, but he could not pry him loose from Clark in Italy. When J. Lawton "Lightning Joe" Collins arrived, having commanded the 25th Infantry Division in the Pacific, Bradley grabbed him. With Ike, he interviewed Collins, questioning him closely about his combat experience. When the Pacific veteran summed up his tactical approach as always targeting the high ground in any attack, Bradley turned to Ike: "He talks our language."[8] Bradley decided right then and there to replace Woodruff with Collins as commander of VII Corps.

To make room for Collins, Woodruff was transferred to the now-vacant command of XIX Corps. Bradley thought of this transfer as temporary. He still hoped that, somehow, Truscott would become available, but, in the meantime, another Pacific war general, Charles H. "Cowboy Pete" Cortlett, arrived. Valuing his experience, Bradley took the personally painful step of sending Woodruff home and putting Cortlett in his place as XIX Corps commander. As for Gerow, Bradley decided to trust his instinct that this fine leader would rise to the demands of corps command in combat.

With these key leadership issues resolved, Bradley worked closely with Eisenhower in reviewing and, ultimately, overhauling the Overlord plan they had been handed. He enthusiastically agreed with Eisenhower that the original plan, which called for an assault by three divisions, packed an insufficient "wallop."[9] Accordingly, he and Ike insisted that it be increased to five divisions supported by much heavier naval gunfire.

Bradley added the proposal that the landings be made at night, a tactic that had worked well in Sicily. The commanders in charge of air and naval assets, however, objected, arguing that pilots and landing craft coxswains would be unable to see their targets and beaches. Bradley's proposal was accordingly rejected, but he persisted in advocating the use of airborne assault to drop men behind part of the landing zone—at night—before the landings commenced. He wanted to use the airborne assault to seize in advance key points of egress from the landing zone and also to wreak havoc in the enemy's rear echelon and transportation and communication networks. He stood almost alone among the senior Overlord commanders in his advocacy of airborne assault, with Trafford Leigh-Mallory, the British officer in charge of tactical air operations, protesting that paratroops deployed at night would suffer 50 percent casualties and glider troops 70 percent casualties. In the end, Eisenhower backed Bradley and insisted on an airborne component, accepting the possibility of heavy casualties. For his part, Bradley worked intensively with the commanders of the two U.S. airborne divisions, the 101st and the 82nd, to plan their assaults.

Bradley was far less successful in his advocacy of Operation Anvil, the proposed secondary landings in southern France, near Marseilles, to be made simultaneously with the Overlord landings in Normandy. With both Marshall and Eisenhower, Bradley believed that Anvil was of critical importance because it would draw off many German defenders from Normandy, it would quickly open up seaports to supply the ongoing needs of the invasion, and it would allow for the immediate participation of Free French forces in the liberation of their own nation. Churchill, Brooke, and Montgomery objected to Anvil because it would require the use of Allied forces that had been earmarked for yet another thrust against Europe's "soft underbelly"—this one in the Balkans. In the end, the Balkan operation was scrapped, but the growing demands of the troubled Italian campaign forced Bradley and Eisenhower to compromise on Anvil. Renamed Operation Dragoon, it was reduced in size and postponed to a month after D-Day.

The final major planning controversy in which Bradley became embroiled concerned the strategic component of air operations. Originally, only tactical aircraft—fighters and light and medium bombers—were slated for use in disrupting the French rail, highway, and bridge networks just prior to and during the landings. Bradley reasoned that heavy "strategic" bombers should also be employed. He believed it critically important to do absolutely everything possible to prevent or to slow German efforts to move troops and, especially, armor and other vehicles to the landing zones. Britain's "Bomber" Harris, along with the U.S. Army Air Forces' Carl "Tooey" Spaatz, clung to the belief that the Allies' strategic air forces should be used exclusively for the strategic bombing of Germany, the destruction of German cities and industry. This, they believed, more than a ground invasion, would ultimately win the war. Accordingly, they strenuously objected to taking the pressure off the German population and German war production by interrupting the strategic bombing campaign to assist tactical fliers in interdicting French trains and destroying French bridges.

On the side of the strategic air advocates was a further objection that intensive strategic bombing would inevitably take a heavy toll on the French civilian population. Whereas tactical bombing could strike surgically, strategic bombing was a blunt instrument. Bradley knew that there was truth to this, and he advocated developing a system that would give civilians some warning of attack. As for the casualties that would nevertheless occur, Bradley deemed them part of the price France would have to pay for its liberation. In the end, working closely with Ike, Bradley prevailed, and the Eighth U.S. Air Force flew some 33 thousand sorties, always with a heavy bomber component, severely crippling the French transportation net. Bradley's willingness to integrate strategic and tactical elements represented a major stride in combined arms doctrine—and one that would influence subsequent American military thinking.

By the time the Overlord plans had reached Bradley, they were intended as a fait accompli, but, little by little, he worked, mainly with Eisenhower, to revise, shape, and refine them. Sometimes he got what he wanted. Often he did not. Yet the more he worked with the Overlord plans, the more his relationships with the top movers and shakers, British as well as American, broadened and matured. He came to know King George VI, Churchill, Brooke, and others. Recognizing his profound strategic differences with Churchill and Brooke especially, Bradley nevertheless came to respect them deeply. The most important evolutionary development was Bradley's working relationship with Eisenhower. Bradley's judgment of his classmate had often been harsh in North Africa and Sicily, and, indeed, Eisenhower made plenty of mistakes in those campaigns, but once Ike assumed principal responsibility for Overlord, Bradley developed a new respect for him. In the end, he attributed to Eisenhower much of the success of the Normandy operation. If Patton tended to regard himself and those around him as characters in some great drama—changeless stock characters, either heroes or villains, either brave men or cowards—Omar Bradley believed in the capacity of people to change and to grow. He seems never to have held a grudge or to have assumed that, because a man erred in 1943, he could not excel in 1944. Most important of all, he believed this of himself as well as others.

Bradley became a close working partner of the famous and the great, yet he never quite lost the Missouri boy's awe of such men. Churchill, King George VI, and others were both delighted and amused when Bradley urged on them his "short snorter," a one-dollar bill on which he collected the autographs of the prominent men with whom he worked. A part of General Bradley emerged as a star-struck autograph hound.

The one figure who did not seem to change was Montgomery. Bradley diagnosed an absence of what he called "chemistry" between him and Montgomery, and what he most resented was the British general's tendency to regard every situation as a stage on which he had to be the star performer. To Bradley's great credit, he understood that it was futile to dwell on these flaws of style and personality, but he nevertheless continued to address specific issues relating to Overlord, especially the breakout phase, the phase of the operation that would follow the landing.

Bradley recalled that Patton was impressed with what Churchill had said about the objective of Overlord: "Remember that this is an invasion, not the creation of a fortified beachhead."[10] Churchill, Patton, and Bradley all understood that Overlord was a prelude to a war of maneuver, a war of movement par excellence. The danger Bradley sensed in Montgomery's stagey pomposity and addiction to method and preparation was precisely a failure to focus on movement, on agility, on improvisation, on recognizing and seizing opportunities as they presented themselves. The map of the breakout plan Monty presented was heavily scored with what he termed "phase lines," precise boundaries indicating the projected extent of the Allied advance on each day following D-Day, the day of the landing. Bradley strenuously objected to the phase lines, arguing that they imposed far too much rigidity on the overall plan and discouraged individual commanders from exploiting evolving opportunity. Moreover, phase lines could not possibly account for unexpected areas of enemy resistance and other imponderable factors. Montgomery responded to Bradley's objections by promising that he would not include the phase lines in the presentation he planned to make to Churchill, Eisenhower, and all the top Overlord commanders on April 7, 1944. Come April 7, however, the lines were still on the map, prompting Bradley to angrily insist that they be removed from the American sector of the breakout plan. The incident was merely a prelude to the many disputes, often rancorous, that would develop between Montgomery and Bradley in the course of the Normandy campaign, the breakout, and, indeed, in all European operations.

+⟩━━⟨+

Intensely skeptical about "Ultra" intelligence during the North African and Sicilian campaigns, Bradley recognized that both British and American intelligence operations had greatly matured in the run up to Overlord, and he eagerly devoured the information that flowed in during the months, weeks, and days before D-Day. He learned enough to fully grasp just what was at stake in the invasion. Years earlier, while umpiring a war game, he had admonished young William Westmoreland always to look at the battlefield from the point of view of the enemy. Now, on the eve of the great cross-Channel invasion, he made himself look at Overlord from the perspective of Adolf Hitler. While others optimistically imagined that Hitler cowered in fear of an invasion, Bradley believed that the Führer regarded it as both a great danger and a great opportunity. If his armies succeeded in throwing the invaders back into the sea, Hitler could be confident that a very long time would pass before another invasion could or would be attempted. That would give him plenty of time to pound England with his V–1s and V–2s, certainly bringing massive destruction and quite possibly forcing a negotiated end to the war—short of an outright victory, perhaps, but an end that might well preserve him in power.

Apart from his big-picture strategic awareness, Bradley was also keenly aware of the formidable nature of the German army defending occupied France. Despite the strain caused by the competing demands of the Russian front, Bradley knew that German forces in the West were something to be reckoned with. His awareness of the enemy, however, also told him that the German commander-in-chief on the ground, Field Marshal Gerd von Rundstedt, sharply differed with his principal subordinate, the legendary Erwin Rommel, on just how to repulse the invasion. Rommel had spent months building up and reinforcing Hitler's vaunted "Atlantic Wall," the massive fortifications along the Channel coast. Although he had gained fame as the Desert Fox—a tank general and exponent of mobile warfare—Rommel thought that a static defense was the best way to stop the invasion. Rommel believed that if the invasion were not halted on the beaches, within the first 48 hours of landing, there would be no stopping it. In contrast, Rundstedt cared little about pushing the invaders into the sea. He believed that a war of maneuver in France would, in the fullness of time, utterly annihilate the Allied armies. Bradley hoped that this difference of very basic opinion would be a fatal weakness in the German defenses, and he intended to do his best to exploit it.

Even as Bradley worked diligently to tie up every loose end before D-Day, he found himself increasingly becoming a celebrity—the "GI General," in Ernie Pyle's phrase; "The Doughboy's General," according to *Time*. The American public had grown uncomfortable with Patton, whose heroism could cross the line into posturing or even brutality, and was eager for a "regular guy" hero. Bradley consistently professed distaste for publicity, but he also believed that, because he was entrusted with the lives of so many of America's sons, the public did have a right to know something about him. Moreover, he managed to take satisfaction in the angle most journalists explored when they covered him, portraying him as an officer who cared about his men, an officer who valued their lives and who would not spend those lives prodigally. Such stories not only comforted soldiers' families, they instilled confidence in the men he sent into battle.

In the days leading up to D-Day, Bradley personally visited as many U.S. units as possible, not only to deliver words of encouragement but, specifically, to allay rumors of inevitably catastrophic casualties. Bradley did not limit his visits to the lower ranks, but also convened his corps and division commanders at Bristol for a final review before embarkation. As one of these commanders, Maxwell Taylor, recalled, "General Bradley, the old school teacher from West Point and the Infantry School, personally conducted the class of generals." Facing the unknown, Bradley fell back upon the familiar—the world not only of West Point and the Infantry School, but of his schoolteacher father. One by one, he called each general up to a map of France, proffered a pointer, and had each man use it to describe in detail his outfit's scheme of maneuver.[11]

To Taylor, the contrast between Patton on the eve of Operation Husky and Bradley on the eve of Overlord was telling. Patton "turned on us with a roar and, waving a menacing swagger stick under our noses, concluded: 'I never want to see you bastards again unless it's at your post on the shores of Sicily.'" Bradley, his classroom lesson concluded, "folded his hands behind his back, his eyes got a little moist, and in lieu of a speech, he simply said, 'Good luck, men.'"[12]

<hr/>

On June 3, 1944, Omar Bradley boarded U.S.S. *Augusta*, the heavy cruiser that had taken FDR to his first historic meeting with Churchill in

Placentia Bay, Newfoundland, back in 1940. There was little to do but wait and worry about all the things over which no human being had any control: the weather, the tides, the light of the moon, the very passage of time itself. Despite a raging storm, early on the morning of June 5, *Augusta* made preparations to steam out into the English Channel.

Bradley was miserable. "The weather was terrible—seemingly too foul for our purposes." Moreover, as he had suffered a painful and embarrassing attack of hemorrhoids just before the Operation Husky landings, so now a "monstrous boil" appeared on his nose, equally painful and embarrassing.[13] Bradley had a navy corpsman lance it, then was obliged to wear a conspicuous bandage lest an infection lay him up at this most critical of times. It was a most unseemly way for a general to lead men into battle.

Bradley comforted himself by donning new experimental infantry boots, manufactured by the Brown Shoe Company of Moberly, Missouri. Despite his multiple anxieties and his bandaged nose, he smiled, his aide Chet Hansen thought, "very lightly as though it is good to be nearer the coast of France and get the invasion under way." Hansen marveled that his boss revealed no "concern or worry whatsoever," but, on the contrary, looked "quite optimistic about the entire operation." Truth be told, Bradley later admitted, "appearances can be deceiving. I was far from optimistic. We were going up against the first team." He also received last-minute intelligence that the German 352nd Division had just moved into the Omaha Beach area, as luck would have it, on training maneuvers. "Omaha was bound to be bloody."[14]

<hr>

For purposes of the assault, a roughly fifty-mile stretch of Norman coast had been divided into five code-named landing beaches: Gold, Juno, and Sword were assigned to the British and Canadians; Utah and Omaha to the Americans. Bradley could do no more than watch the distant action from the bridge of the U.S.S. *Augusta* and monitor a thin stream of communications. Early on, he was gratified and greatly relieved by reports of casualties among the paratroopers who had participated in the nighttime airborne assault he had championed. Fifteen percent were killed or wounded—a considerable toll, to be sure, but far lower than the 50 to 70 percent Leigh-Mallory had predicted. Also coming as a relief were the first reports from Utah beach, which was poorly defended by a single German regiment of reservists and foreign volunteers.

Omaha Beach was another story altogether.

Far more heavily fortified and more fiercely defended than any of the other four beaches, Omaha presented Hitler's vaunted Atlantic Wall at its highest, thickest, and most deadly. The assaulting forces were immediately pinned down, so that, six hours after landing, no more than ten yards of beach had been gained. It was a bloodbath about which Bradley could do absolutely nothing. For some, D-Day was a moment of great glory. For Bradley, the "whole of D-Day was . . . a time of grave personal anxiety and frustration. I was stuck on the *Augusta*." The few real-time reports he managed to glean from the sector gave the "impression that our forces had suffered an irreversible catastrophe."[15] Privately, Bradley pondered evacuating Omaha Beach and redirecting the next invasion wave to Utah Beach or even to the British sector. Such an evacuation would have been both demoralizing and extremely hazardous, but the alternative appeared to be annihilation. Poker player that he was, Bradley kept his fears to himself, waited, and prayed that his men could somehow hang on.

At 1:30 in the afternoon, Bradley received a message from Gerow. The troops that had been pinned down on the beach were now—at long last—advancing up the heights behind it. On the strength of this message, Bradley sent his chief of staff, William Kean, and his aide, Chet Hansen, to reconnoiter Omaha Beach firsthand. They returned with an optimistic report. Enemy fire was still heavy, but progress was undeniable and unstoppable. Bradley abandoned any notion of withdrawing from France—at Omaha Beach or anywhere else. By the end of the day, he was confident that the armies of the United States, Great Britain, and Canada would surely succeed in liberating Europe from its long, brutal imprisonment.

CHAPTER 10

Breakout

Over the next six days, from June 6 to June 12, the Allied invaders welded together their 5 beachheads into an 80-mile-broad lodgment with an average depth of 10 miles. Viewed from the historical distance of more than 60 years, this appears to be a successful classic amphibious assault: hit the beach, seize a beachhead, then penetrate sufficiently to create a lodgment—a firm staging area from which first a breakthrough and then a breakout would be made. The breakthrough would penetrate the enemy's defensive perimeter, and the breakout would widen the breakthrough into a full-out invasion.

To Omar Bradley, close up, the sequence hardly appeared so tidy. What struck him most forcefully, when he ventured ashore on June 7, was the chaos that still prevailed on Omaha Beach, which was littered with the dead and wounded. Somewhere in the back of his mind loomed the awareness that, for all the planning that had gone into the D-Day landings, very little time had been spent on thinking through the breakthrough and breakout phases that had to follow. True, Bernard Law Montgomery had drawn up his irritating "phase lines," but he devoted almost no effort to figuring out just how each of those neatly drawn goals would be reached.

Poker-playing Bradley must have silently struggled to tamp down such swarming doubts so that he could focus on the immediate problems of managing the lodgment. By June 12, eight additional combat divisions had landed. Although Bradley was confident that there was now no chance that the Germans could drive the invaders back into the sea, it was also apparent that resistance was everywhere rapidly stiffening and Bradley surmised that the Allies had a perilously narrow window within which to capture Caen and Cherbourg on the Cotentin Peninsula. These were strategic prizes. Break through Caen, and the invaders would find ideal terrain for a rapid armor advance to Paris, some 120 miles inland. Take Cherbourg, and they would have a large and easily defended channel port from which to keep their operations amply supplied and reinforced. Bradley knew all this, and, what is more, he knew that the Germans—especially Erwin Rommel—knew all this as well.

Tasked with taking Caen, Monty had airily promised that he would do so very rapidly, then would hold the town as the center of a great eastward wheeling movement by the rest of the invasion force. Pivoting on Caen, the First Canadian Army was to turn sharply east-northeast to the Seine, near Rouen. At the same time, the Second British Army would sweep south-southwest of this, through the German strong points of Falaise and Argentan, also driving toward the Seine. First U.S. Army was to provide the major momentum for the breakout, wheeling south past Avranches, from which place it would send forces up the Brittany peninsula, through Rennes, then take Brest on the tip of Brittany; another First Army force would advance toward Nantes on the Loire River, thereby severing Brittany at its neck and isolating it, preventing a German counterattack on the American rear. Two more First Army segments would swing away from Brittany and toward the Seine, one heading for Paris, another aiming south of Paris to close the so-called "Paris-Orléans gap." After George S. Patton Jr.'s Third U.S. Army was activated, it was to move out from Avranches as well and form the easternmost line of advance through the rest of France—and points east.

Such was the big picture. Bradley was all too aware that it was as grand as it was vague. And he was even more keenly aware that it all relied on Montgomery's taking Caen with something approaching the alacrity he had promised. Rommel also saw the big picture. He may or may not have envisioned all of the Allies' breakout intentions, but he clearly grasped that Caen would be the first major battleground and, accordingly, took the high-stakes gamble of transferring three divisions from Brittany to join two divisions already in place to oppose the drive on Caen. As it turned out, this deft action utterly stymied Montgomery by keeping his Second British Army out of Caen for weeks after the landings.

Bradley inwardly fumed at Montgomery, believing that if he had moved more quickly and aggressively, he might have beaten at least some of Rommel's forces to his objective. Now, deprived of Caen, the center of the planned great wheel through France, Bradley concentrated on overrunning the village of Carentan, in the U.S. sector, then deploying three First Army corps to defend a perimeter extending from Caumont to Carentan on the southeastern neck of the Cotentin Peninsula.

So stood the situation as of June 12, when Winston Churchill and Alan Brooke as well as the U.S. Joint Chiefs—George C. Marshall, Admiral Ernest J. King, and Army Air Forces General Henry H. "Hap" Arnold—in company with Ike Eisenhower paid a visit to Normandy. All were in high spirits, including the usually somber Marshall, who predicted that Adolf Hitler could not last much longer and that Germany would almost certainly surrender before Christmas.

Outwardly an optimist, Bradley was always inwardly a skeptic; yet he left no record to suggest that he disputed Marshall's prediction. The fact was that, with the exception of Omaha Beach, the Normandy landings had proceeded much more easily than anticipated, and a good lodgment had been achieved, but the breakthrough was being frustrated at perhaps its most important point—Caen—and Bradley had no clear idea of just how to regain the invasion momentum. Indeed, no sooner had his visitors withdrawn than he received "Ultra" intelligence indicating that Rommel had suddenly shifted the 17th SS Panzer Grenadier Division (along with the 6th Parachute Regiment) from Brittany to the First U.S. Army front, obviously intending to attack newly won Carentan. It was a matter of policy for Bradley to regard Ultra intelligence with a wary eye, but, this time, he swallowed it whole. The blithe high spirits of high command notwithstanding, he understood that the 101st Airborne, which now held Carentan, lacked the heavy equipment to fend off a determined German tank attack. Rommel could readily drive a wedge between First Army's V and VII Corps, perhaps even splitting them clear back to the beaches. At the very least, this would be a major setback; at worst, a catastrophe. Bradley therefore ordered Gee Gerow to send a tank battalion and an armored infantry battalion to Carentan. Thus reinforced with armor, the 101st repulsed Rommel's attack, albeit with heavy losses.

Successful though it was, the repulse scarcely gave Bradley any time for a breath. Transferring Leonard T. "Gee" Gerow's armor to Carentan had weakened the First Army position near Caumont. Coupled with the failure of an Anglo-American attack on German positions at Villers-Bocage, this exposed 1st Division—the Big Red One—dangerously at Caumont. Uncharacteristically quick action by Montgomery, who sent elements of his British 7th Armoured Division to cover the left flank of the U.S. 1st Division, saved the day, buying time for the arrival of more British and American divisions, which dashed once and for all Rommel's rapidly fading hopes for containing the invasion.

In the meantime, north of Carentan, the U.S. VII Corps attacked westward, across the base of the Cotentin Peninsula. But its progress was greatly impeded by the *bocage,* the hedgerows of the Norman coastal farmlands. On June 18, the Americans were able to turn north, and, on June 20, the 9th, 79th, and 4th Infantry Divisions reached the outer defenses of Cherbourg. From June 22 to June 27, the Americans battered Cherbourg's defenses. Once secured, this port became a major avenue of supply for the growing forces of the invasion.

Bradley's June operations on the Cotentin Peninsula were his first bitter taste of hedgerow country. Chiefly in the American sector, the marshy ancient Norman farmlands were crisscrossed by stone walls, typically man-high, completely overgrown with thick, densely tangled hedges. The result was a landscape of unmatched picturesque charm, but also a terrain almost impossible to traverse with tanks, let alone wheeled vehicles. The *bocage* gave all the advantages to the defenders. What is shocking is that Bradley, who had always placed such emphasis on the importance of a commander's thorough knowledge of battlespace terrain, either discounted the *bocage* or totally failed to take it into consideration as he contemplated Normandy operations.

And there was worse to come. As thick as the hedgerows seemed going up the Cotentin Peninsula toward Cherbourg, they were much more formidable obstacles going back down the peninsula, which was precisely where Bradley determined he would make his first major break-through. His tactical preference was always to identify the enemy's soft spot and concentrate his attack there. Bradley believed he saw such a spot on the west Cotentin coast from La Haye du Puits down to the moor-lands of Coutances. Perhaps sight of this opportunity blinded him to the formidable obstacle posed by the *bocage* here. More charitably, we might speculate that Bradley deliberately calculated that the weakness of the Germans in this vicinity would more than compensate for the difficulty of the terrain. In any event, he chose to make a breakout in an area that was a defenders' dream.

In the meantime, as Bradley set up what he hoped would be the de-cisive battle on the west coast of Cotentin, the battle of Normandy devel-oped with great violence elsewhere in the American sector, which, by the end of June, stretched from the west coast of the Cotenin Peninsula east-southeast to Caumont, where the U.S. left flank made contact with the British right. As the Allies continued to race to build up forces behind their lodgment preparatory to the major breakout, the Germans contin-ued to bring up reinforcements in an increasingly desperate bid to stem the invasion. On June 28, SS General Paul Hausser replaced Friedrich Dollmann as commander of the Seventh German Army after Dollmann died under mysterious circumstances at his headquarters (officially, the cause was identified as a heart attack or a stroke, but many believed he had committed suicide by poisoning). Dollmann's death seems to have shaken Hitler, who suddenly lost confidence in Gerd von Rundstedt, overall commander in the West, and, on July 3, replaced him with Field Marshal Gunther von Kluge, who was transferred from the Soviet Front. On this very day, Bradley began his attack southward, down the western

Cotentin coast, but got no farther than Lessay, a short distance south of his starting point, La Haye du Puits.

As Bradley struggled through the *bocage* on his right (Cotentin) flank, his center (mainly XIX Corps) fought fiercely to gain a few miles, finally capturing the important village of Saint-Lô on July 18, though at great cost. By this time, on the left flank of the invasion, the Second British Army finally succeeded in taking at least a part of Caen—the portion west of the Orne River—on July 8. On the 20th, two days after the Americans had captured Saint-Lô, a second British attack took the remainder of Caen, an objective that was supposed to have been achieved almost immediately after D-Day. Thus, as of July 20, the Anglo-American invasion forces held slightly more than 20 percent of the territory they had hoped to possess by this date.

+╼═╾+

As for the portion of the advance Bradley had counted on for a breakthrough—the thrust on his right flank from La Haye du Puits to Coutances—Troy Middleton's VIII Corps was still 12 miles short of the Coutances high ground on July 14 when Bradley ordered him to break off the advance. After a dozen days of very bloody combat, the corps had gained no more than eight miles, total.

Bradley resigned himself to finding an alternative springboard from which to launch the breakout. He also had to reconcile himself to having lost his first battle as an army commander. His defeat had at least three sources. First—perhaps foremost—was the *bocage.* If this failure to take into account terrain is surprising, equally difficult to account for is the second source of defeat, Bradley's underestimation of the quality of the defenders. As a military teacher, he had always cautioned against selling an enemy short, yet, on the Cotentin Peninsula, he did just that. The third source of his defeat was his inconsistency in failing to adhere to his own strategic principles. He had promoted to Eisenhower the idea of the Cotentin advance as a concentrated attack on the enemy's soft spot—and yet, as this operation proceeded, he continued to press an attack along his *entire* front, from the Cotentin coast to Saint Lô, dispersing his forces and thereby reducing his chances of breaking through at any one point.

By the third week in July, Bradley was cudgeling his brains in an effort to work out a new plan for the breakthrough the invaders so desperately needed. At this point, two catalysts lifted his morale and accelerated his thinking. The first was a series of technical developments intended to conquer the *bocage*. These included the use of small explosive charges to blast through the hedgerows, the employment of dozer tanks—ordinary M–4 tanks fitted with hydraulically operated bulldozer blades—and two unique field improvisations. One was a pair of timber prongs fitted on the front of each tank. Dubbed "salad forks," these were used to poke small tunnels into the hedgerows, into which were inserted 15 pounds of explosives packed into the recycled fiberboard containers used to transport 105-mm artillery ammunition. The charge was detonated, blasting a hole into the hedgerow sufficient to allow passage of tanks. The other improvisation became the stuff of legend, an example of the kind of hard-headed can-do ingenuity that helped to make the American GI (including the "GI General") a pop-culture icon in World War II. Using material salvaged from German tank obstacles, Sergeant Curtis G. Culin Jr. of the 102nd Cavalry Reconnaissance Squadron welded a set of steel prongs on the front of a tank to create a device variously called a Culin cutter, hedgerow prongs, hedgerow cutters, and a Rhinoceros; the tanks fitted with these were universally dubbed Rhinos. Bradley saw a demonstration of the Culin cutter on July 14 and was impressed. He thought it superior to the salad fork because it required no explosives, but simply plowed through the hedgerows. He immediately ordered First Army Ordnance to build as many Culin cutters as possible, using "Rommel's Asparagus," steel antitank obstacles salvaged from the Normandy beaches, as raw material. By July 25, more than 500 tanks had been fitted out as Rhinos. Most historians today believe that the role of the Rhinos has been exaggerated, and that they were hardly a panacea for the hedgerow problem. Nevertheless, the Rhinos and the other innovations were significant advances in coping with terrain that had proved a deadly frustration.[1]

The second catalyst was human rather than technological. It came in the person of George S. Patton Jr., who arrived in France early in July.

Day after day, he anxiously waited for Third Army to be activated. On July 20, when the news broke that Adolf Hitler had narrowly escaped death from an assassin's bomb in his "Wolf's Lair" headquarters, Patton called at Bradley's headquarters: "For God's sake, Brad, you've got to get me into this fight before the war is over. I'm in the doghouse now and I'm apt to die there, unless I pull something spectacular to get me out!"[2]

It was the kind of selfish outburst—as if the war existed for the personal glorification of George Patton—that had prompted Bradley to encourage Eisenhower to send him home. Now, however, it was precisely this nothing-to-lose frame of mind that seemed to Bradley the human equivalent of the salad fork and the Rhino. Bradley needed a breakthrough. Patton's glory-hungry leadership might just be sufficiently explosive to give him one.

Bradley had been working on Operation Cobra, a new approach to the Normandy breakout. Instead of attempting an advance along a broad front, he decided to concentrate on a 6,000-yard front 5 miles west of Saint-Lô. Coordinating with air, he would call in an intensive bombing against German positions, use infantry to tear a gap into the bomb-weakened defenders, then roll through with armor and mechanized units to the west coast of the Cotentin Peninsula, targeting the area between Coutances and Brehal. This would cut off the German LXXXIV Corps, which held the highway between Saint-Lô and Perriers-Lessay. Along this road, the breakthrough could continue—and be expanded into a general breakout.

"Cobra," Patton wrote in his diary on July 23, "is really a very timid operation . . . [but] it is the best operation which had been planned so far, and I hope it works."[3]

+≈══≈+

Operation Cobra was scheduled to step off on July 21, but a thick cloud cover grounded the bombers. The 22nd and the 23rd were also heavily overcast, and Bradley fretted that the Germans would discover his build-up and that he would thereby lose the element of surprise. After weather officers predicted a clear day for July 24, Bradley authorized the bombers to take off from their English bases; but when clouds persisted over the target areas, he directed the bombers to turn back. The attack would have to be postponed to July 25. Tragically, one group of heavy bombers failed to get the message and dropped their ordnance through the clouds—directly on the U.S. 30th Division, inflicting heavy casualties.

What distressed Bradley more than the fact that the bombers had not received the recall message was that they had approached their target not on a course parallel to the ground troops, but perpendicular to them, flying over the heads of the soldiers. When the bombs were dropped short, they fell on friendlies. In preparing the air component of the assault, Bradley had been at pains to avoid precisely this by specifying that the bombers would make an approach parallel with his advancing column. He had secured agreement on this, but now—*after* the accident—Air Chief Marshal Sir Trafford Leigh-Mallory explained to him that the promised parallel approach had proved impossible because it would have taken more than two and a half hours to funnel the heavy bombers along the narrow course prescribed. Bradley understood—but he was outraged that this had not been anticipated in planning. He believed he had been deliberately deceived, and now, seething with rage, he was faced with having to authorize—this time with his full knowledge—a second extremely hazardous carpet bombing very close to his own lines.

"Shall I tell them to go ahead in the morning?" Leigh-Mallory asked.

"We've got no choice. The Boche will build up out front if we don't get this thing off soon. But we're still taking an awful chance. Another short drop could ruin us." Bradley paused, then made his decision: "Let it go that way. We'll be ready in the morning."[4]

The morning of July 25 dawned. The very air, Bradley wrote, "throbbed with heavy bombers while I fidgeted . . . within easy reach of the telephone. . . . The thunder had scarcely rolled away when the casualty reports began trickling in." Handing Bradley a teletype, Truman C. "Tubby" Thorson, one of his long-time staff officers, grimly announced: "They've done it again."

Bradley cried: "Oh Christ, not another short drop?"

Thorson nodded. Among the several hundred killed was the universally respected General Lesley McNair, who had journeyed to the front, eager to see the results of the Stateside training he had been directing.

This latest mishap cast a pall over Cobra, and Bradley went to bed on the night of July 25 thinking that the operation would prove an abortive failure. In fact, as the air attacks continued through July 26, the infantry advanced according to plan, sending battered German defenders into full retreat. On the morning of July 27, seeing the German line break under the infantry, J. Lawton "Lightning Joe" Collins, commanding VII Corps, knew the time had come to throw in his armor—just as Bradley had planned.

The tanks roared through the broken lines of retreating German troops. Omar Bradley had his breakthrough.

Seizing on what he saw as a developing new opportunity, Bradley hurriedly rewrote operational orders at noon on July 27. Originally, VII Corps was to advance to Coutances, cutting across VIII Corps' route of advance. Now he ordered both corps to roll down the Cotentin together, pushing all the way to Avranches. He was intent on quickly capturing that town and, moving through it, overrunning Brittany.

Up to this point, Patton had been waiting in the wings, and up to this point, Bradley had gotten along without him. Now, however, having achieved a faster and bigger breakthrough than he had imagined possible, Bradley wanted Patton's immediate help in turning it into a full-scale breakout into Brittany. Third Army would not be activated until August 1, but Bradley, on July 28, asked Patton to assume unofficial command of Middleton's VIII Corps until that date. For all his misgivings about Patton, Bradley intended to harness his proven ability to move men and machines forward. Middleton was competent and stable, a slow and steady engine suited to heavy hauling. Patton was volatile and brilliant, a hot machine fit for racing. That was what Bradley wanted now.

Historians of World War II have frequently pointed out that Patton regarded Operation Cobra as timid. Rarely, however, do they go on to observe that, by July 28, in a letter to Eisenhower, he commented that "Bradley certainly has done a wonderful job," complaining that his "only kick is that [Bradley] will win the war before I get in." On the 29th, when he was already unofficially commanding Middleton's corps, Patton noted in his diary that "Bradley came up . . . and told me his plans. They are getting more ambitious but are just what I wanted to do . . . so I am very happy . . . I think we can clear the Brest [Brittany] peninsula very fast. The thing to do is to rush them off their feet before they get set."[5] The same historians who have highlighted Patton's criticism of Bradley's "timid" Cobra plan give Patton all the credit for transforming it into the ambitious operation that launched the Twelfth U.S. Army Group's magnificent advance across France and into Germany. But the fact is that Patton joined Cobra—at Bradley's invitation and insistence—only after Bradley himself had begun to expand the operation. Indeed, it is clear that Bradley saw Patton as the very man he needed to ensure that Cobra would be expanded as much as it possibly could. Did Patton "transform" Cobra? Yes. But the fuller answer is that *Bradley* deliberately employed Patton to transform Cobra. It was the beginning of synergistic relationship compounded of opposite personalities. Bradley would use Patton, and, for his part, Patton was only too happy to be used.

On the evening of July 30, an element of the 4th Armored Division, part of Middleton's corps, entered Avranches. It held on precariously through the night, receiving reinforcements on July 31. From Avranches, Patton sent the 4th and 6th Armored Divisions through the gap that had been created between the German left flank and the coast. The German commander von Kluge reported in some panic to his boss, Field Marshal Alfred Jodl, that the "whole western front has been ripped open."[6] On August 1, as Patton officially assumed command of Third Army and Bradley took command of Twelfth U.S. Army Group (consisting of the First and Third Armies, soon to be joined by the Ninth), Bradley ordered Patton to secure the Avranches exit from the Cotentin Peninsula, then to turn west into Brittany.

Almost immediately, Bradley had reason to vent considerable irritation with Patton's broad interpretation of these orders. The Third Army commander sent Middleton's VIII Corps (now a part of Third Army) deep into Brittany without regard to protecting his rear or flanks. On August 2, Bradley visited Middleton's command post. The worried corps commander pointed to his map. "I hate to attack with so much of the enemy at my rear, especially while it's so exposed. If the other fellow were to break through at Avranches to the coast, I'd be cut off way out here in Brittany."[7]

Bradley understood instantly. "Dammit," he said. "George seems more interested in making headlines with the capture of Brest [on the Brittany coast] than in using his head on tactics. I don't care if we get Brest tomorrow—or ten days later. Once we isolate the Brittany peninsula, we'll get it anyhow. But we can't take a chance on an open flank. That's why I ordered George to block the peninsula neck."[8]

Bradley then drove out to Patton's command post.

"For God's sake, George, what are you going to do about this open flank of Troy Middleton's? I just ordered the 79th down there [to protect the flank]. But I hate to by-pass an Army commander on orders to a corps."[9]

Clearly, Bradley expected a showdown. Instead, Patton "smiled sheepishly" and put his arm around Bradley's shoulder.

"Fine, fine, Brad. That's just what I would have done. But enough of that—here, let me show you how we're getting on."[10]

It was a telling exchange. With good reason, Bradley distrusted Patton, but yet still needed him. He was a very powerful weapon—and, like all powerful weapons, his recoil packed a painful kick. Yet Patton also possessed a childlike charm. If Bradley had been genuinely fed up with Patton, he would have bridled under the patronizing arm and the cooing "Fine, fine, Brad." Instead, he let himself be charmed.

For the rest of the war in Europe, the press would often portray Patton and Bradley as rivals. Bradley always claimed that this was a media fabrication. Undeniably, however, the two generals were indeed dramatic foils: the loose cannon versus the steady hand, the commander with the gleaming helmet versus the one who humbly wore GI olive drab. Undeniably as well, Bradley would frequently complain about Patton—the complaints growing louder, more specific, and more frequent in remarks and writings after the war. Yet, throughout the European campaign, Bradley never again suggested, let alone asked for, Patton's relief. Instead, Bradley tolerated him, tolerated him so that he could exploit him as a raw and mighty engine of advance, however heedless.

CHAPTER 11

Crisis

Popular treatments of World War II in Europe typically highlight two great events: D-Day (along with Operation Cobra) and the Battle of the Bulge. Between these two points the story is often told as one of inexorable Allied advance, marred only by Bernard Law Montgomery's overreaching in the Netherlands at Arnhem with Operation Market-Garden.

Glib to be sure; nevertheless, there is an element of truth in this telling, for the Allied advance—particularly that of Omar Bradley's Twelfth U.S. Army Group—that followed Operation Cobra was indeed spectacular. Yet, in addition to leaving out numerous crises, this version of history fails to address the remarkable fact that, even as they moved across France, the Allies had not agreed on many aspects of their basic strategy. Montgomery, in command of the Twenty-first Army Group and (until September 1, 1944) chief ground-force commander, resolutely advocated a dagger thrust attack aimed at penetrating German defenses along a narrow front, whereas Bradley backed Eisenhower's broad-front strategy. The two approaches were never fully reconciled, with the result that Ike grudgingly approved Monty's tragically flawed Market-Garden dagger thrust as well as elements of Bradley's broad-front strategy.

The fiasco of Operation Market-Garden, which spanned September 17 to September 25, 1944, marked the low point in relations between Montgomery and his American colleagues, especially Omar Bradley; however, the split between Bradley and Montgomery had begun earlier and was associated with the ever-increasing synergy between Bradley and George S. Patton Jr. Insofar as Eisenhower, as supreme Allied commander, saw his role as harmonizing and unifying the Anglo-American war effort, the Bradley-Patton odd couple sometimes found itself in opposition not only to Montgomery but to Eisenhower as well.

On August 7, 1944, the Germans counterattacked American positions near the hard-won town of Avranches, launch point of the Normandy breakout. The enemy succeeded in penetrating the gap between Courtney Hodges's XIX and VII Corps, overrunning the town of Mortain. From here, the Germans advanced to Juvigny and Le Mesnil-Tove, where they were stopped by the U.S. 30th Division, which was supported by air attacks. Having already anticipated a German move in the Avranches area, Bradley was ready with a counter-counterattack, using a mixture of infantry and armor. Not only did Hodges's First U.S. Army hold, an armored counterattack at Mortain drove the Germans back by August 12, making way for First Army to begin its general eastward breakout into France.

Bradley instantly grasped that the collapse of the German attack on Avranches had significantly weakened the enemy position by isolating its attacking force west of the main body of the German army. Seeing an opportunity to encircle the enemy west of Argentan and Falaise, Bradley coordinated with Montgomery an action in which British and Canadian forces would break through at Falaise and link up with U.S. forces approaching Falaise from the opposite direction. The aimed-for result was a double envelopment designed to cut off and bag a large number of Germans. This was, in fact, such a good idea that Montgomery, Patton, and Eisenhower, in addition to Bradley, all claimed credit for it.

For his part of the encirclement, Montgomery relied on Canadian forces to take Falaise. Unfortunately, they proved incapable of making good progress, and by August 12 they had yet to reach the town. In the meantime, the American component of the operation, the XV Corps of Patton's Third U.S. Army, under Wade Hampton Haislip, reached its assigned objective, Argentan, leaving a gap, centered on Falaise, between Argentan and the Canadians. On his own, Patton authorized Haislip to exceed Montgomery's orders and advance all the way to Falaise and, if necessary, beyond it, all with the purpose of closing the "Falaise gap" in order to prevent the withdrawal of the encircled Germans. Haislip hesitated because he believed that he lacked sufficient forces to move that far ahead without aid from the Canadians. Patton then turned to Bradley, asking for his express authorization to push on to Falaise.

Doubtless, Bradley expected such a request from Patton, but he was not yet prepared to allow him either to risk the exposure of such an advance or—equally important—to openly defy Montgomery. At this point, Bradley was still fully committed to remaining loyal to the concept of Anglo-American cooperation. He therefore ordered Patton to hold at Argentan and build up forces there. Whereas Patton wanted to surround more and more Germans, Bradley, concerned that that portion of the enemy already partially contained would break out and get away, ordered him to prepare to tie off the sack farther down its neck. The catch would be smaller for this, but still substantial.

In the end, German defeat in the so-called Falaise gap was severe, yet it is also true that considerably more of the enemy escaped encirclement than had been anticipated. Patton was disappointed, and although he directed a modicum of his bitterness against Bradley, he hurled far more against Montgomery.

For his part, Bradley did not view Patton's aggressive ambition with nearly as disapproving an eye as he had in the past. Officially, Bradley knew what his job was, and, also officially, he knew he had done his job in holding Patton at Argentan. But, as he reflected on it, he came to believe that, in doing what he was *supposed* to do, he had almost certainly diminished the magnitude of victory. Like Patton, Bradley became increasingly critical of Montgomery. To the degree that the Falaise encirclement had been flawed, it was, Bradley wrote late in life, "a shattering disappointment—one of the greatest of the war. A golden opportunity had truly been lost. I boiled inside, blaming

Monty for the blunder. . . . His unrealistic faith in the Canadians had cost us the golden opportunity."[1]

The rift between Bradley and Montgomery widened precisely at a time of growing nationalism among both the American and British public. Bradley's elevation to Twelfth Army Group command had been, like Eisenhower's assumption of direct command of Allied ground forces on September 1, fully planned in advance. Yet the way the American press played up both developments made it seem as if they constituted a *demotion* for Montgomery. The British press picked up on this theme and amplified it. With these stories in the air, war correspondents, always looking for a more dramatic angle, manufactured an active and intense rivalry between Bradley and Montgomery. This translated to presenting the Allied advance as a horse race between the British and the Americans. Bradley always portrayed himself as both sufficiently modest and sophisticated as to never allow himself to be swayed by the press. And perhaps his change in attitude after Falaise really did have nothing to do with the newspaper stories. But, whatever the cause, he came increasingly to think of himself as an American commander rather than an Allied one. It is abundantly clear that he had grown to doubt Montgomery as a war strategist, but it is also evident that he had grown weary of sacrificing the prestige of the U.S. Army on the altar of British strategy.

<hr />

As of the beginning of September 1944—in the wake of Falaise—Bradley's Twelfth Army Group had liberated Paris and, in concert with Montgomery's Twenty-first Army Group, had pretty well swept the German army out of France; even though part of Brittany remained occupied, German forces here were effectively cut off and therefore neutralized. On the right (south) of the Twelfth Army Group's advance, Patton's Third Army was poised to fight for the ground between the Moselle and Saar Rivers, while, on the left (north), Hodges's First Army was about ready to cross into Germany itself.

Despite the lingering disappointment of Falaise, the Allies at this stage were afflicted with what Eisenhower called "victory fever," a heady combination of exhilaration and complacency. Virtually alone among his colleagues, Bradley professed to be immune. Brittany stuck in his craw, not for strategic reasons—isolated, it was now all but irrelevant—but for what it said about the German will to continue the fight. While most of his fellow commanders believed that the back of the Wehrmacht and the Waffen SS had been broken, Bradley had apparently learned a valuable lesson from the earlier failure of his campaign in the Cotentin Peninsula. He was not about to sell the enemy short, reasoning that if the Germans held out stubbornly at Brest, they would defend that much more fiercely the Rhine River.

Bradley harbored no serious doubt that the Allies would prevail. For him, the question was not if Germany would be defeated nor even when that would happen, but just how that foregone conclusion should be brought about. As Allied high command saw it at this moment in the war, four avenues of advance into Germany presented themselves. On the right (south) of the Allied front—the front covered by Patton's Third Army—advance into Germany was possible from Metz to Frankfurt via Saarbrücken. In the center (north of Patton's Third Army), Hodges's First Army could roll into Germany due east, straight through the Ardennes. If Hodges and Montgomery (whose front was to Hodges's left, or north) made a combined advance, they could do so by skirting the Ardennes around its northern face, proceeding into Germany via Maubeuge and Liege. The northernmost route, through the Flanders plain, was exclusively Montgomery's. All four routes offered access to the Ruhr valley, the industrial heartland of Germany on which war production—indeed, virtually all German production—depended. From the Ruhr, the way to Berlin was open and obvious. The Allied assumption was that to capture the Ruhr was to seize the heart of Germany, and to take Berlin was to have its head as well.

Eisenhower favored the approach north of the Ardennes, in Montgomery's sector. This irked Bradley, who, like Patton, was coming to believe that Ike was far too much the Anglophile; nevertheless, Bradley found it impossible to dispute at least one of Ike's two main strategic reasons for this choice. His first reason, however, Bradley found dubious. Ike liked the northern approach in part because the principal concentration of German troops was in the north. He wanted to attack strength. For Bradley, who favored exploitation of the enemy's softer spots, this was an argument *against* attacking at that point. As for the second reason—that an advance in Montgomery's sector would involve capturing Antwerp, a key port—Bradley had to admit it was absolutely sound. For the realtor, the mantra is *location, location, location;* for the general (Bradley firmly believed) it should be *logistics, logistics, logistics.* Besides, Eisenhower's proposal of a subsidiary thrust, to be made by Patton's Third Army east via Metz, made the plan somewhat more palatable.

Yet, to the consternation of both Bradley and Eisenhower, Montgomery was not satisfied with all that Ike proposed to give him. He continued to advocate what he called his "single-thrust theory" over what he denominated as Ike's "broad front policy." Montgomery believed that one narrow thrust across the Rhine and into the heart of Germany was the quickest way to win the war—provided that the thrust was backed by the whole of the Allied armies. In effect, Montgomery proposed himself as sole candidate for conqueror of Germany. He wanted all supplies and resources diverted to him, with every other commander and command existing only to support him and his. That meant that he could not tolerate even a secondary thrust by Patton.

Officially on an equal footing with Montgomery, Omar Bradley had no desire to play second fiddle to him, especially considering that U.S. forces in Europe now outnumbered the British and that the Third Army was a mere 30 miles from Metz and just 70 from the Saar River, apparently facing little resistance all the way to Germany's last-ditch "Western Wall" defenses, which, according to Allied intelligence, were weakly manned at that time. It would be easy to conclude that a contest of wills had developed between the egocentric Montgomery and the self-effacing Bradley, but it was far bigger than that. There was a question of national prestige, to be sure; but, even more, Bradley believed it a strategic sin to waste the gains Patton had made. In the end, on September 4, Eisenhower ordered Montgomery's Twenty-first Army Group, together with two corps of Hodges's First U.S. Army, to secure Antwerp and breach the portion of the Siegfried Line covering the Ruhr. This accomplished, the army would seize the Ruhr. Simultaneously, Patton's Third Army, together with one corps of the First Army, was to occupy the portion of the Siegfried Line covering the Saar and then capture Frankfurt. Eisenhower's order specified that troops operating against the Ruhr northwest of the

Ardennes—Montgomery's command—were, above all else, to be ensured adequate support.

Thus Ike fully authorized two operations, but Montgomery's was to be given top priority. Nevertheless, Bradley saw enough wiggle room in Ike's orders to encourage—and enable—Patton to do as much as possible. Bradley reasoned that adequately supporting Montgomery's northern thrust meant allocating 5 thousand tons of supplies to the First Army (two corps of which were under Montgomery) versus just 2 thousand to Patton's Third. So much was clear. However, on September 2, Eisenhower was returning from a visit to Bradley's command post when his light liaison plane, a single-engine L–5, made a forced landing on the beach near his command villa on the French coast at Granville. (Stunningly enough, the villa was named "Montgomery.") Seeing that the tide was coming in, Ike helped the pilot push the aircraft up the beach to higher ground, in the process twisting the knee he had badly injured during his West Point football days. The result was the supreme commander's almost complete immobility during the opening phase of the advances in the north and the south. Perhaps Bradley consciously took advantage of his chief's incapacity by deciding to divide supplies not 5 thousand/2 thousand tons, but equally between First and Third Armies. He also gave Patton authorization to cross the Moselle and force the Siegfried Line. Moreover, Bradley transferred V Corps from Hodges's First Army to the Third to cover Patton's left (northern) flank as he pushed toward the Saar.

On September 17, in a letter to his son George, Patton wrote: "We got Nancy . . . but Metz which is one of the best fortified cities in the world is still holding out." In his diary, Patton recorded that "Bradley called to say that Monty wants all the Americans to stop so that he, Monty, can 'make a dagger-thrust with the 21st Army Group at the heart of Germany.' Bradley said he thought it would be a 'butter-knife thrust.'" Clearly picking up on Bradley's contempt for his British colleague, Patton conspired with his commanding officer. We can gather the gist of the exchange between the two American commanders from the rest of Patton's diary entry for September 17: "To hell with Monty. I must get so involved [in operations] that they can't stop me. I told Bradley not to call me until after dark on the 19th. He agreed."[2]

Bradley understood very well what Patton was about. The Third Army commander would order a reconnaissance in force (tantamount to an offensive advance) for the explicit purpose of provoking a battle. Once the battle had developed, he would of course have "no choice" but to commit fully to it. For his part, Bradley would be able to report to Ike—in perfect innocence—that Patton, deeply involved, would *have* to be supported, lest he suffer defeat.

Bradley's conspiracy with Patton is defensible on strategic grounds. First, Patton was ideally positioned for a productive thrust at a time when German forces in this area were reportedly at their most vulnerable. Second, General Patton was not an asset to be wasted in the relative idleness of a supporting role. Yet the full extent of Bradley's contempt for Montgomery and his "dagger-thrust"—Operation Market-Garden—and of his own willingness to defy Eisenhower becomes fully apparent only when we recognize that, even as he authorized Patton's advance to the Moselle, he also ordered an attack on Brest, still in German hands far to the rear of Allied lines. By this time, the remaining German presence in Brittany, including in the port of Brest, was irrelevant because these forces were utterly isolated. Both Bradley and Patton were well aware that Brest no longer held strategic importance. Nevertheless, Bradley committed Troy Middleton's VIII Corps—80 thousand men—to capturing the city. Not only did Middleton incur 10 thousand casualties, killed or wounded, in the operation, he consumed supplies that otherwise would have been available to Montgomery. The commander who, in Sicily, had been outraged by what he saw as Patton's monomaniacal obsession with beating Montgomery to Messina—even after Messina had ceased to be a strategically critical objective—now willingly expended men and treasure to take another mere prestige objective.

Did Bradley's defiance of both Montgomery and Eisenhower hurt the Allied cause? It is impossible to say. Patton advanced, but was bogged down in a heavy fight at Metz. Montgomery's Operation Market-Garden overreached and failed with heartbreaking losses. History has generally laid the blame for this defeat entirely at the feet of Montgomery and his plan, yet it is also true that Bradley was unavailable to support him, and Hodges, heavily engaged at Aachen on the German frontier, could offer no support either. Thus Monty was left entirely to his own devices, and when, in mid-October, it was decided to make a new effort to cross the Rhine before winter, Montgomery loudly proclaimed that success—*this time*—would depend on Bradley's refraining from major action south of the Ardennes.

Bradley dismissed this caveat as Montgomery's groping for an excuse to explain away the failure of Market-Garden. More important, Ike rejected it as well. While the supreme Allied commander refused to disallow the continuation of Patton's advance in the south, he reconfirmed that the major thrust should be in the north against the Ruhr, but he decided that, this time, it would be the First and Ninth U.S. Armies that would make the thrust—and they would be under the command not of Bernard Law Montgomery, but of Omar Nelson Bradley.

+═══+

Bradley positioned both the First Army (under Hodges) and the Ninth (under William H. "Big Simp" Simpson) before the Aachen gap, which was the most immediate entryway into Germany. The First was to advance toward Cologne, while the Ninth targeted Krefeld. Another strategic consideration of this positioning was to separate Montgomery's army group from the First U.S. Army by inserting the Ninth between them. Montgomery had a seemingly irresistible habit of incorporating American forces into his command, and Bradley feared that First Army staff had become so embittered against Montgomery that they would mutiny if they were again forced to serve under him. Moreover, should Montgomery appropriate some American forces, Bradley wanted him to have a piece of the relatively inexperienced Ninth Army rather than the seasoned veterans of the First.

Despite the careful thought that had gone into Bradley's strategy, with regard both to the Germans and to Montgomery, the First and Ninth Armies faced enormous obstacles of terrain. There was the dense Huertgen Forest, which, like the Norman *bocage*, gave all the advantages to the defenders, and there was the Roer River, with seven dams, the two largest of which, if blown by the Germans, would bring floods that would make crossing the lower Roer virtually impossible. Somewhat belatedly, Bradley realized the importance of gaining control of the Roer dams and spillways, and, on November 2, sent the 28th Division (reinforced with artillery and engineers) to attack the town of Schmidt, partly to gain the two big dams. Yet even in this attack, Bradley—who had worked so hard in the States to master battle terrain—underestimated the difficulty of the rugged ground. This problem was amplified by heavy mining of the roads. Whereas General Norman "Dutch" Cota could not get his tanks through to where he needed them, the Germans, approaching from the east, easily could. Worse, bad weather grounded all air support. Cota was soundly defeated by the German 11th Panzer Division, reinforced by two more divisions.

Despite the defeat and the risk still posed by the Roer dams Bradley bulled ahead with his Rhine offensive. At this point, he had yet to set a date for Patton's Third Army, south of the Ardennes and the First and Ninth Armies, to make its attack. Eisenhower had specified that it would step off only when logistics permitted. Patton, however, urged Bradley to give him the green light immediately. Doubtless anxious himself to get a successful advance moving, after the repulse of the 28th Division, Bradley complied, authorizing Patton to begin on November 8. In contrast to the beautiful conditions that had favored Third Army in the breakout following Operation Cobra, miserable late fall weather brought mud, floods, and a dearth of air support. Hailed as a commander who ate up enemy real estate, Patton was now bogged down.

In the meantime, the force of four corps from First and Ninth Armies began their Rhine advance north of the Ardennes. By the third week in November, this advance was also bogged down in a vicious Huertgen Forest firefight, which lasted through the end of the month and cost First and Ninth Armies some 35 thousand casualties. Although many thousands of Germans had been killed or captured, the Rhine—and the industrial Ruhr basin—still lay far ahead. By early December, the worst European winter in some three decades was settling in. All expectations of victory by Christmas were dashed, and what had begun as a race across France was now a slog, even a stalemate.

━━━

It was a dangerous time—for the Allies as well as for Omar Bradley. There was no serious concern that the war would be lost, but the longer it took to win, the greater the danger of yielding to the temptation to accept something less than Germany's unconditional surrender. Moreover, the sooner the war in Europe was won, the sooner troops could be released for service in the Pacific in the great planned invasion of Japan. The danger to Bradley was more immediate. The baton of principal command had been passed to him after Montgomery's Market-Garden had failed. Now that Bradley was on the ropes, Montgomery chimed in by pointing out that the theater naturally divided into two fronts, one north of the Ardennes, the other south of it. He pushed for a single commander to coordinate both—meaning, of course, himself. And he continued to advocate the narrow-front, dagger-thrust approach.

Considerations of leadership—Was Montgomery a better commander than Bradley after all?—and nationalism aside, Montgomery was right. Bradley's operations had distended Twelfth Army Group so that it was no longer a truly cohesive force, whereas Montgomery's Twenty-first Army Group remained formed and poised for an advance. All things being equal, it made strategic sense at this point either to put both sides of the Ardennes under unified command or to allow Montgomery to make a new dagger-thrust attack in the north. But all things were not equal, and questions of leadership and nationalism abounded as they never had before. Eisenhower tried desperately to talk the next step out with his commanders. During this process, Allied momentum, already eroded by weather, terrain, and unexpectedly resolute German resistance, was yet further diminished.

Ike and Bradley—and, doubtless, Montgomery, too—agonized, yet, for them, the issue remained not whether the endgame would or would not be played, but just how to play it. The prevailing assumption was that the German army was a defeated force that simply had not yet surrendered. Despite their many frustrations, the Allied commanders indulged themselves in the belief that they were victors in the process of choosing the appropriate mode of their victory.

Into the resulting gap of Allied attitude and momentum, the German army suddenly and shockingly thrust itself.

On December 16, 1944, 25 German divisions burst through the morning fog and descended upon Troy Middleton's VIII Corps, First U.S. Army, which had been moved out of Brittany and was now providing a thin cover for the Ardennes in Luxembourg, near the town of Bastogne. This had been a quiet sector, and for that reason Bradley held it lightly with five green or battle-weary (and recuperating) U.S. divisions. Bradley was surely aware that, in 1940, the French had gambled on what they deemed a sure thing—the Ardennes presented such a formidable obstacle, the mechanized German army would never invade through it. He was also aware that the French had lost that bet—and France into the bargain. Yet something of that same reasoning entered into his decision to leave the Ardennes lightly defended in December 1944.

In fairness to Bradley, no one in Allied command expected the "defeated" German army to launch a major offensive anywhere, let alone the difficult ground of the Ardennes. Bradley believed this failure of expectation and imagination was compounded by two additional factors. The first was the assumption that Gerd von Rundstedt was calling the shots, and would therefore maintain his armies in a militarily rational, strategically predictable defensive posture. "No one came forward to say, 'Hey, watch yourself. Hitler may really be in charge. Anything can happen.'"[3] The second was that old bugaboo, overreliance on "Ultra" intelligence, which did not pick up any radio or telephone traffic indicating a major operation. Apparently, no one thought the Germans would plan and launch a major operation under total radio silence.

In a strategic climate that fostered disbelief in the willingness and ability of the German army to launch a major offensive, Bradley interpreted the initial assault as what he called a "spoiling attack," a harassment of relatively little consequence. The tendency to dismiss it as such was amplified by the distance that lay between Bradley's headquarters in Luxembourg City and Middleton's position before the Ardennes. Nor did the attack move Bradley to inspect the VIII Corps situation personally. Indeed, he even decided that there was no reason for him to cancel his plans to go to Versailles for a scheduled meeting with Eisenhower. The inclement weather that prevailed during this period—greatly aiding the Germans in their attack on Middleton's weak position—made flying impossible, so Bradley had to be driven to his meeting. It was evening by the time he reached Versailles, and it was there, at an even greater remove from the Ardennes, that he and Ike received word that the German penetration was no spoiling attack, but the thrust of a major offensive—some

200 thousand men against little more than 80 thousand Americans—which was forcing a massive salient, or "bulge," into the VIII Corps sector. It was this that would give the offensive its popular name: the Battle of the Bulge.

Late in the evening of December 16, Bradley phoned Patton from Versailles. He ordered the Third Army commander to immediately send his 10th Armored Division to Middleton's aid. Patton had just resumed his own eastward drive and protested that he could hardly afford to part with a division now. Even though Patton himself had earlier remarked the vulnerability of Middleton's position, he was now so intent on his own advance that he, too, dismissed the German action as a spoiling attack. Bradley responded by giving Patton a direct order to send the 10th. "Bradley admitted my logic," Patton wrote in his diary on December 17, "but took counsel of his fears and ordered the . . . move. I wish he were less timid." Yet even the impulsive Patton thought better of it after a moment's reflection: "He probably knows more of the situation than he can say over the telephone."[4] With that, Patton lost no time in obeying Bradley's order and had the division moving within the hour.

That night, Bradley lay sleepless, not because he had been caught unawares, but because he was excited by the possibility of converting the German offensive into a massive German rout.

＋════╬╬

Thus far, the Germans had exploited all the advantages that terrain afforded a defender. Now assuming the offensive, they were exposing themselves, forsaking the advantages of terrain, rendering themselves vulnerable. This terrifying fiasco might yet be turned into the triumph that would break the stalemate that had prevailed since late September. Fortunately for Bradley—and the Allied cause—Patton's attitude almost instantly metamorphosed from resentment over having to interrupt his advance to a proactive commitment to what he, too, now perceived as the potential of turning the German offensive into the devastation of the German army. On December 17, without awaiting further orders from Bradley, he began preparations for a massive and rapid reinforcement of the Ardennes, summoning his III Corps commander, John Millikin, to tell him that he would likely be required to turn on a dime and move north in order to lead a counterattack.

On the 18th, Patton arrived at Bradley's Luxembourg headquarters and established himself there, working closely with Bradley throughout the entire Battle of the Bulge. Bradley had resolved that, in order to convert the German offensive into an American one, all other ongoing offensive attacks would have to be broken off. Hodges's First Army would have to be turned from the east to the south, and Patton's Third from the east to the north. As soon as Patton arrived, Bradley told him: "You won't like what I'm going to do, but I fear it is necessary," then outlined this radical change of direction.[5] To his delighted relief, Bradley found that, instead of protesting, Patton was already on his very page. When Bradley asked him what he could do to help Middleton right away, Patton astounded him by replying that he could have the 4th Armored Division and the 80th and 26th Infantry Divisions on the march north within 24 hours.

On the next day, December 19, Eisenhower convened a meeting at Bradley's main headquarters in Verdun. Although skeptical that even Patton could redeem his bold pledge, Bradley asked him to come to the Verdun meeting.

Eisenhower, whose fighting spirit both Bradley and Patton had frequently doubted, rose to the occasion with electrifying brilliance. His G–2 (intelligence officer) opened the meeting with a grim outline of the Ardennes situation. Ike allowed him to finish, then stood up to make a statement intended to neutralize everything that had just been said. "The present situation," he declared, "is to be regarded as one of opportunity to us and not of disaster. There will be only cheerful faces at this conference table." Patton took this as an invitation to speak out: "Hell, let's have the guts to let the _____ _ _____ go all the way to Paris. Then we'll really cut 'em off and chew 'em up." Ike and everyone else—except, possibly, Patton himself—took this as a joke, and grim faces suddenly broke into grins. A smiling Ike proclaimed that, no, the enemy "would never be allowed to cross the Meuse."[6]

Ike asked Patton when he could attack. He gave the supreme Allied commander the same answer he had given Bradley. He could attack on December 22, with three divisions: the 4th Armored and the 26th and 80th Infantry. Whereas Bradley had responded with quiet skepticism,

Ike snapped out: "Don't be fatuous, George. If you try to go that early, you won't have all three divisions ready and you'll go piecemeal. You will start on the twenty-second and I want your initial blow to be a strong one! I'd even settle for the twenty-third if it takes that long to get three full divisions."[7]

Patton held his ground, insisting that he could make an effective attack on the 22nd. At this, some of the British officers at the conference table laughed as others nervously shuffled their feet. Then, realizing that Patton was in earnest, many suddenly straightened in their chairs. Bradley remained silent, content to let Patton speak for himself. Swallowing his doubts, Eisenhower approved Patton's proposal, setting 0400, December 22, as the time for an attack by III Corps of the Third Army.

+≡≡≡≡+

Put strictly in terms of summary military history, the story of the American response to the Bulge may be quickly told. Patton not only relieved the 101st Airborne Division and 10th Armored Division, which were surrounded at Bastogne, he also enabled Hodges to realign his First U.S. Army, transforming his posture from defense to counterattack.

Patton's timely arrival thwarted Sepp Dietrich's advance in the north, but, for a time, Hasso von Manteuffel, at the German center, continued his drive, and Adolf Hitler authorized other units to throw their support to him. Manteuffel got as far as the village of Foy-Notre Dame, a mere three miles east of the Meuse River, on December 24. Two days earlier, however, the weather, which had been socked in and stormy, broke sufficiently to allow the Allies to call in air support. Massive sorties on December 23 and December 24 disrupted German supply lines, which had already been stretched to the breaking point, and Manteuffel's advance to Foy-Notre Dame forever marked the farthest extent of the "bulge."

Manteuffel was pounded by Hodges from the north and assailed by the defenders of Bastogne. On January 3, Hodges's VII Corps attacked southward against Manteuffel's position as elements of Patton's Third Army inexorably advanced northward. The intention of the two Americans was to crush Manteuffel in a pincers movement, but the weather turned foul again, greatly slowing the advance of both Hodges and Patton. By the time they converged on Houffalize on January 16, Manteuffel had withdrawn. With his escape, the opportunity to destroy most of the German units committed to the Ardennes Offensive had been lost. Despite this, the Americans inflicted some 100 thousand casualties against an attacking force of 500 thousand, crushing the final major German offensive of the war. Hitler's bold gamble at the Ardennes had resulted in the loss of many of his irreplaceable combat-worthy reserves and the near destruction of the Luftwaffe.

Such a summary, however, tells only a fraction of the story. Early in the contest, on December 19, Allied panic was still so intense that, when Montgomery proposed his taking over command of all Allied forces north of the Ardennes—that is, all of Hodges's First Army and most of Simpson's Ninth—Ike listened and let himself be persuaded. Late in the evening, Eisenhower's chief of staff, Walter Bedell "Beetle" Smith, telephoned Bradley, arguing that turning over the First and most of the Ninth to Montgomery would "save us a great deal of trouble, especially if your communications with Hodges or Simpson go out." Bradley later confessed to being "completely dumbfounded—and shocked," in large part because Smith had always been one of Montgomery's harshest critics.

In his posthumously published autobiography, Bradley wrote that he felt as if Ike were slapping him in the face and admitted that he should have stood up to Smith, telling him that Supreme Headquarters Allied Expeditionary Forces (SHAEF) was "losing its head" and that he had things under control. Instead, he "knuckled under." Bradley called the result—giving Montgomery operational control of two of his three armies—"the worst possible mistake Ike could have made."[8]

What Bradley did not report in his autobiography is that he had stood up to Ike himself. Insisting that Smith put him through to Ike, Bradley shouted into the telephone: "By God! I cannot be responsible to the American people if you do this. I resign." He did not "knuckle under," but neither did he calmly make a rational case for retaining control of the First and Ninth U.S. Armies. Instead, he made it personal and came on with uncharacteristic petulance. Ike responded harshly: "Brad, I—not you—am responsible to the American people. Your resignation means absolutely nothing!"[9]

As Bradley saw it, the conservatism of Montgomery ensured the failure of an opportunity to cut off the German salient—to pinch off the "bulge"—high up at its neck, thereby achieving what had not been achieved at the Falaise gap: the destruction of the greater part of the German army. For the "souls of the dead American GI's, whose stubborn courage had already doomed the German offensive," Bradley could now only pray. And for himself, the general and the man, he regarded these as "the darkest of times."[10]

CHAPTER 12

Victory

Two major crossroads loomed as great prizes in the area of the German Ardennes offensive, the towns of St. Vith and Bastogne. Now that Bernard Law Montgomery had assumed operational command of the First and Ninth Armies, St. Vith was in his sector and was therefore his problem. Bastogne, probably the less important of the two towns, was in George S. Patton Jr.'s Third Army sector and, therefore, Bradley's concern. He immersed himself in Patton's remarkable and heroic efforts to reach and relieve the encircled Belgian city. Among some military historians there is a belief that Omar Bradley was largely irrelevant to the ultimate victory at Bastogne and that it was entirely Patton's show. Yet a balanced view must credit Bradley's single-minded insistence that the city be held even as it credits Patton's combat leadership in holding it.

As for the course of the Battle of the Bulge north of Bastogne, both Bradley and Patton fumed at what they saw as Montgomery's fatal conservatism, which, they believed, bordered on defeatism. On Christmas night, after a meeting in which the British commander (Bradley later wrote) had been "more arrogant and egotistical than I had ever seen him . . . lecturing and scolding me like a schoolboy," Montgomery wrote Field Marshal Alan Brooke: "I was absolutely frank with [Bradley]. I said the Germans had given us a real 'bloody nose'; it was useless to pretend that we were going to turn this quickly into a great victory; it was a proper defeat and we had better admit it . . . I then said it was entirely our own fault." By that, Montgomery meant that it was Bradley's and Eisenhower's fault, because they insisted on a broad front strategy rather than his own "dagger-thrust" approach: "[W]e had gone much too far with our right [that is, with Patton's advance]; we had tried to develop two thrusts at the same time, and neither had been strong enough to gain decisive results. The enemy saw his chance and took it. Now we were in a proper muddle."[1]

Throughout his Christmas-night meeting with Monty, an enraged Bradley held his tongue. Restraint, which he considered a requirement of military professionalism, was a hallmark of Bradley's dealings with colleagues and even superiors when he believed that a showdown might gain him emotional satisfaction but would fail to win the day. However, after suffering Monty's insolence in silence, Bradley called "Beetle" Smith the next morning, pointing out to him that, by going on the defensive, Montgomery was throwing away a great opportunity to inflict a decisive defeat on the Germans. This said, Bradley made his move, directly asking for the return of First and Ninth armies, so that he could get results in the north just as he was getting from Patton, in the south.

Leaving his conversation to simmer with Smith and his boss, Ike, Bradley took the extraordinary step of deliberately circumventing the chain of command. He wrote a letter to First Army commander Courtney Hodges, who was under Montgomery's operational orders. Conceding that he, Omar Bradley, no longer controlled First Army and that, therefore, the letter was not to be considered a directive, Bradley nevertheless told Hodges that he did not view the situation "in as grave a light as Marshal Montgomery," but he viewed with alarm any plan Montgomery might present that involved giving up ground that could be favorable to future operations. Bradley concluded by advising Hodges to "study the battle with an eye to pushing the enemy back 'as soon as the situation seems to warrant.'"[2]

Fortunately for Bradley—and, his partisans would say, for the Allies generally—two positive developments on December 26 bolstered his aggressive counterpoint to Montgomery's defensive conservatism. The first was Patton's penetration of the German lines around Bastogne, opening a corridor to the besieged 101st Airborne and 10th Armored Division. The second was the initiative of Ernest Harmon, who took his 2nd Armored Division on the offensive against the leading westbound Panzers of Rundstedt. Completely destroying the 2nd Panzer Division, Harmon brought the German westward advance to a halt. In blatant defiance of Montgomery's directives, J. Lawton "Lighting Joe" Collins, commanding VII Corps, had ordered Harmon to leave his defensive position near Dinant and go on the attack. Harmon's success prompted Collins to draw up plans for a counteroffensive designed to cut off the "bulge" at its waist, thereby bagging a large number of the enemy.

These successes, combined with the pressure Bradley had put on SHAEF via Smith, moved Eisenhower to convene a meeting with both Bradley and Montgomery on December 27. Bradley decided to prepare by calling on Ike beforehand, but discovered that he had already left for Brussels, the place appointed for the meeting, so Bradley spoke instead to Smith once again.

"Damn it, Bedell, can't you people get Monty going in the north? As near as we can tell the other fellow's [i.e., the enemy] reached the highwater mark today. He'll soon be starting to pull back—if not tonight, certainly by tomorrow." As Bradley saw it, the chance to destroy much of the German army was in danger of slipping away, just as it had at the Falaise gap. Patton thought enough of the importance of the meeting to make a note of it in his diary on the 27th: "Bradley left at 1000 to see Ike, Montgomery, and Smith. If Ike will put Bradley back in command of the First and Ninth Armies, we can bag the whole German army." Montgomery's relentless conservatism had caused Patton to evaluate his American colleagues on an entirely new scale: "I wish Ike were more of a gambler, but he is certainly a lion compared to Montgomery, and Bradley is better than Ike as far as nerve is concerned. . . . Monty is a tired little fart. War requires the taking of risks and he won't take them."[3]

A Luftwaffe bomb damaged the train Ike had been scheduled to take to Brussels, forcing him to postpone the meeting for a day—but also giving Bradley a chance to see him first, at SHAEF headquarters in Versailles, without Montgomery present. To Ike and others, both British and American, Bradley offered no criticism or complaint, but instead presented comprehensive strategy proposals for both the short and long term. In the short term, he pushed Collins's idea of an immediate pincer attack against the waist of the "bulge": Patton would attack out of Bastogne, toward the northeast, while Hodges, using Collins's VII Corps as a spearhead, would attack southeast. Seizing as homely an analogy as he could find, Bradley declared that this "would put the cap on the toothpaste tube and trap the bulk of the German Army."[4] As for the long term, Bradley proposed changing Allied strategy substantially in order to exploit the overreaching blunder that Adolf Hitler had made with the Ardennes offensive. Bradley wanted the main Allied effort to be shifted from the north—and from Montgomery—to the central portion of the front, which was, of course, his own sector. First and Third U.S. Armies would move eastward, abreast, and relentlessly pursue the retreating German armies through the Eifel region and into the area of Bonn. After crossing the Rhine, the advancing armies would use armor to exploit the open country that stretched between Frankfurt and Kassel. Simultaneously, Montgomery, to the north, would also cross the Rhine, operating mainly to protect the left flank of the two American armies. Jake Devers, commanding Sixth Army Group, would be held in a defensive position along the Saar.

The main advantage Bradley promoted with his long-term strategy was speed: the operation could be launched almost immediately, and it would put so much pressure on the Germans that they would be unable to pause long enough to form a strong defensive line against the continued Allied advance. Moreover, as with D-Day, a center drive defied German expectations. Whereas in the cross-Channel invasion, the Germans had expected a landing at Pas-de-Calais, so now they anticipated the main Allied thrust to come in the north.

Ike authorized the short-term pincers operation immediately, but he announced that he would withhold his formal decision on the long-term strategy until after meeting with Montgomery. Nevertheless, he let

Bradley know that he was not himself sold on it. Unwilling to risk another "bulge"—a deep enemy penetration against a thinly held portion of front—he favored instead creating a strong and easily defended line from which the main attack into Germany could be launched. And that main attack, he persisted in thinking, should be up north and under Montgomery, with William H. "Big Simp" Simpson's Ninth Army as reinforcement.

That's where Ike began. But in the course of talking this out further with Bradley, he reversed himself and tentatively decided after all to adopt a version of the center strategy, albeit with a strict caveat. Unless the strategy produced early evidence of decisive success, he would break off the attack, whereupon the First and Third Armies would go on the defensive in support of a shift to Montgomery in the north.

Bradley had won First Army back from Montgomery, but he pushed for at least temporary repossession of the Ninth as well, which he said could assist in his central push. Ike refused, complaining that he was under so much pressure to put Montgomery in command of *all* ground forces that he dare not take too much away from him.

On December 28, Ike, without Bradley, met with Montgomery. Predictably, the British commander raised strong objections to Bradley's long-term strategy, vehemently insisting that all fronts except his own assume a defensive posture in support of his solo "dagger-thrust" into Germany. Ike listened, then returned to SHAEF—this time relatively unmoved by Montgomery's by-now repetitive arguments. He repeated his authorization of Bradley's short-term pincers attack and added authorization of the modified version of the long-term strategy, using First and Third Armies in a broad advance at the center of the Allied front. For this, First Army would be returned to Bradley's command; Ninth Army, however, would stay with Montgomery.

Eisenhower's backing of Bradley provoked an unbending response from Montgomery, who imperiously demanded that the center-thrust advance be canceled, effectively admonishing Ike to bear in mind that Bradley had failed at the Battle of the Bulge and offering himself as the only viable candidate for overall command of the main drive into Germany. He made these remarks against a background of heightened nationalism in the American and British press. The rhetoric in the papers grew so partisan that General George C. Marshall, fed up with British popular opinion, cautioned Ike to make "no concessions of any kind whatsoever" to Montgomery.[5]

The contest of wills between Montgomery and the top American commanders had become a question of numbers, and the numbers were now on the side of the Americans: U.S. forces in Europe substantially exceeded those of Britain. When Montgomery delayed committing two Ninth Army corps to coordinate with Patton's attack against the neck of "the bulge," Ike, bolstered by Marshall's letter to him, prepared to force a showdown. Either he or Montgomery would have to step down, and seeing that the U.S. Army now constituted the main force in theater, there seemed little doubt that Montgomery would have to do the stepping. Before it came to this, however, Montgomery blinked. He vowed to cooperate.

⊹⊱══⊰⊹

The Anglo-American armistice that resulted from Monty's pledge proved short lived, but hostilities were renewed not so much because of anything Bradley or Montgomery deliberately did, but because of a new round of nationalist news stories in the British press calling for Montgomery's appointment as top ground commander. Genuinely alarmed that the Anglo-American alliance might buckle under the weight of a press campaign he did not authorize, Montgomery tried, on January 7, 1945, to restore amity with a press conference aimed at making a plea for Allied solidarity. That certainly sounded like a good idea—and Bradley even believed it was well-intentioned on Montgomery's part—yet the self-portrayal Monty presented at the press conference ultimately served to suggest that, at the Battle of the Bulge, he and he alone had saved the Allied cause, not to mention rescued the American army.

Bradley and his staff heard the press conference at second hand, through a story broadcast by the BBC. It was sufficient nevertheless to prompt one staff officer, Ralph Ingersoll (in civilian life, the founder-publisher of the leftist New York daily *PM*), to write: "Gentle Omar—for the first, last and only time in the campaign—got all-out right-down-to-his-toes mad." Once again, he threatened to resign, telephoning Eisenhower and announced point-blank: "I cannot serve under Montgomery. If he is to be put in command of all ground forces, you must send me home, for if Montgomery goes in over me, I will have lost the confidence of my command. . . . This is one thing I cannot take." Days earlier, Bradley had told Patton that he would feel obliged to ask for relief rather than allow Twelfth Army Group to go to Montgomery. "George clasped me by the arm. 'If you quit, Brad, then I'll be quitting with you.'"[6] Before he ended his phone call to Ike, Bradley let him know about this exchange.

Eisenhower assured Bradley that Montgomery was not going to become ground commander, and he further promised to call Winston Churchill and also to ask that the British press to end its divisive rabble rousing by clarifying the Bulge story as well as the Allied command set-up.

That should have been sufficient, but Bradley allowed his staff to persuade him to hold a press conference of his own, which he did on January 9—without the knowledge, let alone the approval, of Eisenhower. Bradley frankly defended his strategy in the Ardennes campaign, explaining that leaving the sector lightly defended had been a calculated risk. He even sniped: "Had we followed more cautious policies we would still be fighting west of Paris."[7] Eisenhower let Bradley's uncharacteristic press conference pass without comment, but he himself never unambiguously denied the rumor that the transfer of operational command of the First and Ninth U.S. Armies to Montgomery during the Bulge had been much more than a move to improve communications, that it had been, in effect, Bradley's partial relief from command. And because Ike let the rumor stand, it persists, with significant credibility, both within unofficial army lore and among a number of military historians.

In the end, it was rotten weather more than Montgomery's caution that slowed the Allied response to the threat of the "bulge." The result was still a conversion from stunned American defeat into a major Allied victory, but, because the cap was not screwed onto the toothpaste tube as quickly as Bradley had wanted, a significant portion of the German army was able to withdraw, battered but intact. The Battle of the Bulge hurt the Germans, but it did not kill them.

Nevertheless, with the Ardennes campaign closed, Eisenhower and his lieutenants turned to the Rhine in full earnest. It would be an advance across a broad front, with the Twenty-first Army Group (under Montgomery) crossing in the north, Bradley's Twelfth Army Group in the center, and, in the south, the Sixth Army Group (under Devers and consisting of the French First Army and the Seventh U.S. Army) performing mainly in a defensive role, but authorized to cross the Rhine as the opportunity presented itself. Preparatory to the crossings, Twenty-first Army Group was to implement Operations Veritable and Grenade, and the First U.S. Army—in Bradley's army group—was to execute Operation Lumberjack, all intended to clear the Rhine approaches.

On March 2, elements of the Ninth U.S. Army (operating as part of the Twenty-first Army Group) became the first Allied units to reach the west bank of the Rhine, opposite Düsseldorf. Their crossing was delayed, however, because the Germans had destroyed all of the bridges and because Montgomery insisted on making time-consuming preparations for the crossing, so intricate, elaborate, and massive that Bradley believed they rivaled the preparations for D-Day. While the preliminaries were in progress, and even as Montgomery demanded that Bradley hold ten First Army divisions in reserve as a precaution against a reverse, elements of the First Army discovered that the Germans had failed to demolish the Remagen Bridge. On March 7, without ceremony, they seized the bridge and began crossing the Rhine River.

First Army commander Hodges phoned Bradley to tell him.

"Hot dog, Courtney. This will bust him wide open. Are you getting stuff across?"

"Just as fast as we can push it over."

"Shove everything you can across it, Courtney, and button up the bridgehead tightly."[8]

Bradley later confessed to being "engulfed with euphoria"—apparently not so much because the crossing of the river signified the imminence of final victory over the Germans but because one of *his* armies had beaten Montgomery by a matter of weeks.

Harold "Pink" Bull, Ike's assistant chief of staff—who was present at Bradley's headquarters when he took Hodges's telephone call—objected to the idea of exploiting the Remagen crossing because, he said, "it's in the wrong place. It just doesn't fit the plan. Ike's heart is in your sector but right now his mind is up north."[9]

Bradley was furious with disbelief. Turning to Bull, he spat out: "What in hell do you want us to do, pull back and blow it up?"[10] With that, he picked up the phone to tell Ike about the crossing.

"Brad," the supreme Allied commander responded, "that's wonderful."

Bradley then told Eisenhower that he wanted to push across everything he had in the area. Ike replied: "Sure, get right across with everything you've got. It's the best break we've had."

Now, fixing his eyes on Bull, Bradley told Ike that his assistant chief of staff was opposed to exploiting Remagen because it did not fit "the plan." Ike exploded: "To hell with the planners. Sure, go on, Brad, and I'll give you everything we've got to hold that bridgehead."[11]

In fact, the supreme Allied commander imposed a limit of five divisions for the Remagen crossing. This made sense, given Eisenhower's broad-front policy. He wanted to develop multiple bridgeheads up and down the Rhine before effecting a full crossing of any one Allied force. But Bradley feared that Montgomery would exploit this limit to draw away Twelfth Army Group units once his own Twenty-first Army Group finally crossed the river. On March 9, therefore, Bradley conferred with his army commanders and shared his concern. For Patton, it was so much preaching to the choir. His diary entry for this date reflects what were presumably Bradley's own remarks: "It is essential," Patton wrote, "to get the First and Third Armies so deeply involved in their present plans that they cannot be moved north to play second fiddle to the British-instilled idea of attacking with 60 divisions on the Ruhr plain." Patton recorded that "Bradley was anxious for me to coordinate with [Alexander] Patch [commanding a corps of Sixth Army], but since he cannot jump [the Rhine] until the 15th, I am going to attack as soon as possible, because at this stage of the war, time is more important than coordination."[12]

Once again, Bradley and Patton became co-conspirators, and, on March 10, while Montgomery's Twenty-first Army Group continued preparations to cross the Rhine at Wesel, north of the Ruhr, Patton and

Patch feverishly finished clearing the region between the Moselle and the Rhine (while the First French Army—under Jean-Marie de Lattre de Tassigny—dealt with German resistance in the so-called Colmar Pocket). From March 22 to 23, Patton established a bridgehead at Oppenheim, south of Mainz, beating Montgomery across the river by a day. On the 24th, the main body of the First Army crossed, but instead of conforming to Montgomery's Twenty-first Army Group and striking out north, toward the Ruhr, it headed east and southeast, en route to a link-up with Patton's Third Army at Giessen. On March 28, the armies of Patton and Hodges broke through German resistance and made a deep sweep via Frankfurt, penetrating east of the Ruhr. Simpson's Ninth army—still under Montgomery's operational command—descended on the other side of the Ruhr, linking up with elements of the First Army at Lippstadt, thereby encircling and cutting off the 350 thousand German soldiers of Field Marshal Walther Model's army group. It was precisely the kind of "bag" that had eluded Bradley at Falaise and at least partially eluded him at the Battle of the Bulge.

With the Rhine crossings and the great gains made in the Ruhr, Bradley broke free not only of German resistance, but of the strategic anchor Montgomery had come to represent. At the start of the year, Bradley's spirits, along with his military reputation, were at low ebb. Now both soared, as did his stock with the American public and—of more immediate importance—Ike Eisenhower, who eagerly turned to him for advice on the closing phase of the endgame.

━━━━

Throughout the European campaign to this point, the overriding Allied strategy, especially as it emanated from the supreme Allied commander, had been to destroy the German army. That statement is not nearly as self-evident as it appears. For the alternative to this strategy was to conceive of the campaign as liberating cities, towns, territories, and nations. But so strongly was Ike Eisenhower driven by the military objective of destroying the enemy army that, in August 1944, he fretted at being obliged to *divert* forces to liberate Paris, which he did grudgingly, regarding it as a political objective that was very much secondary to the far more critical military one. Also throughout the European campaign—to this point—Omar Bradley had functioned less as a strategist than as a grand tactician, whose business it was to devise and implement the means of carrying out the prevailing strategy of killing the enemy army. After the Rhine crossings, however, Eisenhower effectively elevated Bradley to the loftiest of strategic realms by asking him to participate—with Winston Churchill, Alan Brooke, Montgomery, and himself—in the final planning for the conquest of Germany. As it turned out, Bradley played such a prominent role in formulating the final strategy that, in his World War II memoir, *On to Berlin,* James Gavin referred to the war's culminating plan as "the Bradley Plan." In his own autobiography, Bradley demurred—albeit only somewhat: "While it is true that my contribution to the plan was substantial, it is not accurate to grant me sole authorship. The major features . . . were jointly conceived by Ike and me, and accepted without major dissent by Hodges and Patton in a meeting with Ike and me at Remagen on March 26."[13]

Even if Bradley had been the sole author of the endgame strategy, it was fully in keeping with the strategy that had guided everything preceding it. And therein lay the source of the controversy the "Bradley Plan" created as well as the world-altering effect it had.

Throughout the entire European campaign, one Anglo-American goal seemed too obvious to debate: the eventual conquest of Berlin. Yet, like the liberation of Paris, that goal was actually at variance with the basic Anglo-American strategy of killing the enemy army, as opposed to taking territory. As Bradley and Ike pondered the endgame, they returned to that basic strategy.

When Eisenhower asked Bradley what he thought it would cost to break through from the Anglo-American position on the Elbe to Berlin, he shot back with an estimate of 100 thousand casualties, calling it "a pretty stiff price to pay for a prestige objective, especially when we've got to fall back and let the other fellow take over." In the past, Bradley had used the expression "the other fellow" to refer to the enemy; now he meant the Soviets. Not only were they much closer to Berlin (as of March 26, 1945) than any of the Anglo-American forces—30 miles as opposed 190 miles, in the case of the Twenty-first Army Group—but it had already been decided politically, at the Yalta Conference (February 4–11,

1945) and in a subsequent London meeting of the European Advisory Commission, that Berlin would be occupied as a four-power enclave within the portion of Germany designated as the Soviet zone of occupation. Bradley later noted that the isolation of Berlin deep in the Soviet zone made it a poor objective and went against a major logistical tenet: "In fighting a battle I would never have assumed responsibility for a sector unless I was certain I could have supplied it. In the supply of Berlin we were to be totally dependent upon the good will of the Soviets. And dependence, I learned as a boy in Missouri, does not make for the very best neighbors."[14] In Bradley's view, Berlin was simply not worth the taking, even if that meant conceding it to the Soviets.

Yet another factor entered into the Eisenhower-Bradley decision to allow the Soviets to take Berlin while the Anglo-American effort concentrated on territory to the south. Intelligence reports from the Office of Strategic Services (OSS)—precursor of the CIA—and "Ultra" decrypts strongly suggested that Hitler and a cohort of fanatical Nazis, including the core of the government as well as a large force of loyal Waffen SS troops, intended to retreat to a "redoubt" in the Austrian Alps to make a final suicidal stand against the Allied invaders. According to this intelligence, Hitler's mountain retreat above the village of Berchtesgaden would serve as the headquarters of the "Nazi redoubt." Bradley, who had always professed a healthy skepticism in interpreting intelligence—especially intelligence heavily derived from "Ultra" intercepts and decrypts—did not hesitate to believe this information. Both he and Ike were persuaded that a failure immediately to clean out the redoubt might drag the war out for months as fanatical Nazis, holed up in the Alps, took a heavy toll on American troops, and brought the war to an uncertain and unsettled conclusion, leaving the potential for a resurgence of the Nazi cause.

As Bradley and Eisenhower conceived it, the endgame plan called for the Twelfth Army Group—with the Ninth Army finally restored to Bradley's operational command—to complete the encirclement of German forces in the Ruhr and make a general link up with the westbound Red Army forces at the Elbe River. Jake Devers's Sixth Army Group would protect Bradley's right (southern) flank while getting into position for a drive into Austria, and Montgomery's Twenty-first Army Group (less the Ninth U.S. Army) would protect Bradley's left (northern) flank as well as drive across the Elbe in the north, all the way to the Danish border.

The plan unmistakably cast Montgomery in a supporting role and, predictably, elicited a howl of protest from the field marshal as well as the British generally, who not only decried the "demotion" of Montgomery, but also the relinquishment of Berlin to the Soviets. Ike remained steadfast against the British onslaught.

Earlier in the campaign, Bradley had overcome his distrust and disapproval of Patton in order to forge a powerful synergy with him. It was clear that he had also resolved any differences he had with Eisenhower, especially now that Ike stood up against the British. Bradley staff officer Ralph Ingersoll believed that Eisenhower's spine had been stiffened by none other than Bradley, who had become "so completely the boss that Eisenhower had no choice but to approve" of Bradley's plan to bypass Berlin. Moreover, Ingersoll thought that Bradley's strategy at this point had been inspired by the example of one of his military idols, William Tecumseh Sherman. Bradley wanted a drive that would split Germany in two, much as Sherman's drive through Georgia had split the Confederacy.[15] This, not occupation of the capital, would ensure the destruction of all German military resistance, Bradley concluded.

⊢═══⊣

Whatever the full extent of Bradley's authorship of the European endgame, there can be no doubt that he was fully committed to the plan and that—for better or worse, as far as postwar relations with the Soviets would go—it was this plan that carried the European campaign to final victory.

Bradley was in his last World War II operational headquarters, at the Hotel Furstenhof in Bad Wildungen southwest of Kassel, when the telephone rang at about 5 A.M. on May 7.

It was Ike.

"Brad, it's all over."[16]

That was it. Bradley instantly notified the commanders of his four armies—armies totaling 1.3 million men, the largest field force any American had ever commanded—to tell them that the German surrender would be effective as of 0001, May 9, 1945. In contrast to World War I, in which General John J. Pershing had ordered his commanders to keep their men fighting (and dying) until precisely the time of armistice—the eleventh hour of the eleventh day of the eleventh month of 1918—Bradley ordered his generals "to hold firmly in place and risk no more casualties."[17]

It was an order typical of the "GI General," who confessed that, even as Ike's *It's all over* continued to reverberate in his ears, his "mind was awash with images and sensations [of] that large, blood-drenched swath of Europe [on which] 586,628 American soldiers had fallen—135,576 to rise no more." He did not return to sleep after Ike's call that early morning in May 1945—"I could hear the cries of the wounded, smell the stench of death"—yet he closed his eyes nevertheless "and thanked God for victory."[18]

CHAPTER 13

Five Stars

During the headiest days of the Normandy campaign, when it seemed that the war could not possibly last past Christmas 1944, Omar Bradley had asked General George C. Marshall to ensure his transfer to the Pacific at the conclusion of the European war. As the fighting in Europe ground down, Marshall did recommend Bradley to Douglas MacArthur, who replied that he did not intend to use *any* army group commanders—other than himself, of course. Marshall, in turn, sent a letter to Eisenhower, asking if Bradley wanted to serve under MacArthur as an army (rather than an army group) commander. The suggestion infuriated Eisenhower, because it amounted to what he deemed a very public demotion, which might (among other things) diminish Bradley's vital "influence in the post-war army." Only after he had finished dictating most of his angry reply to Marshall did Ike think to call Bradley to get *his* feelings on the matter. Bradley's only response was "I will serve anywhere in any position General Marshall assigns me."[1]

Marshall wrote Eisenhower on April 27 that he would not ask Bradley to serve as a Pacific army commander. If Ike now looked forward to keeping Bradley with him to aid in the bewildering and multifarious tasks of the occupation of Germany, his expectations were dashed in a matter of weeks. On May 17, Eisenhower summoned Bradley to his headquarters at Reims, waved a War Department telegram in front of him, and announced, "Brad, before I show you this, you had better pour yourself a good stiff drink."[2]

Bourbon in hand, Bradley read the cable, which explained that President Harry S. Truman, having serious problems with the Veterans Administration, asked Marshall to release Omar Bradley to serve as head of the VA for at least a year or two.[3]

Bradley was devastated by news of this non-operational, bureaucratic assignment, and Eisenhower was moved to soften the blow. He promised Bradley that unless President Truman insisted on his becoming army chief of staff, he would decline the job in Bradley's favor. If Ike could see no way of avoiding the job, he would accept it for only two years instead of the customary four and only on condition that Bradley would replace him.

Thus bucked up, Bradley said yes to President Truman and returned to the States on June 2 to a hero's welcome. After a month's leave with his wife, Mary, he reported to the VA in mid-August, by which time Hiroshima and Nagasaki had been leveled by atomic bombs, and World War II was over.

Amid national V-J Day celebrations, Bradley assumed his new duties in Washington. To reporters he put the very best face on his assignment, saying that he did not "think there's any job in the country I'd sooner not have nor any job in the world I'd like to do better. For even though it is burdened with problems, it gives me the chance to do something for the men who did so much for us."[4] Over the next two years, he forged a solid working relationship with his fellow Missourian, Truman, and radically reorganized and revitalized the chronically underfunded, inadequately staffed, and generally feeble VA medical system. He used his war-won popularity to make allies in the press, and he used his integrity and character to gain passage of a massive VA funding bill.

When Bradley left the VA at the end of 1947, he could proudly quote Lois Mattox Miller and James Monohan, medical journalists writing for *Reader's Digest,* who declared that in "two years" he had "transformed the medical service of the Veterans Administration from a national scandal to a model establishment." At the end of his life, Bradley wrote that he had been compelled him "to send hundreds of thousands of men into battle," he had heard "the mournful cries of the wounded," and he had "seen the maimed stoically enduring nearly unbearable pain. Nothing I have done in my life gave me more satisfaction than the knowledge that I had done my utmost to ease their way when they came home."[5]

+┣══╡+

As Ike had promised, Bradley was named U.S. Army chief of staff, succeeding Eisenhower on February 7, 1948. He was faced with the job of fitting the army into the newly created Department of Defense, which had replaced the old War Department and under which all of the services, now including an independent U.S. Air Force in addition to the army, navy, and Marine Corps, were unified under a single secretary of defense—the brilliant and beleaguered James Forrestal, who, Bradley predicted, was doomed to work himself to death. On May 22, 1949, while being treated at Bethesda Naval Hospital for "nervous and physical exhaustion," Forrestal leaped to his death from his room's window.

For Bradley, Forrestal was a man to be admired, but also a cautionary tale about how not to let a big job kill you. Bradley accordingly reorganized the Army General Staff so as to free up the chief for high-level strategic planning and consultation with the secretary of defense and other officials. Routine work was handled by men in three positions Bradley created: a vice chief of staff, who oversaw two deputy chiefs, one for plans and operations, the other for administration. The strategic issues that faced Bradley were those of the newly begun "Cold War," which necessitated his making a delicate transition from thinking like the commander of an army group committed to total, all-out war, to a chief of staff shaping policy and strategy for carefully metered military responses, for deterrent defense, and for "limited war," all pursuant to the "containment policy" of the so-called Truman Doctrine: the idea that the United States would oppose the aggressive expansion of Communism wherever and whenever it appeared in the world, yet do so without igniting World War III.

Bradley was the first in what would be a long line of chiefs of staff who had to learn to plan for and to manage limited conflicts and brush-fire wars. Unlike many of his successors, however, he was additionally burdened by the combination of a daunting mission and a shrinking budget. Indeed, he found himself in a through-the-looking-glass world, expected to perform as the senior officer of an army big and tough enough to oppose the Soviets, yet without the men or means to present a credible military presence. Demobilized and defunded, the army, Bradley believed, had become an administrative organization without real combat effectiveness.

In the most precarious of situations and times, Omar Bradley became the first American general obliged to think in truly global terms. Yet, in contrast to George C. Marshall during World War II, a conflict that dominated all aspects of American life, including politics, Bradley was not called on to originate strategy so much as to administer the strategy dictated by Cold War politics—and to do so as best as could be done with what was now severely constrained military forces. He therefore concentrated on the "salvage"—it was *his* word[6]—of the army, even turning down Eisenhower when he asked him if he would accept the post of chairman of the Joint Chiefs of Staff (JCS).

At the time he asked Bradley this question, in early 1949, Eisenhower had taken a leave of absence from the presidency of Columbia University to answer President Truman's call to serve in the temporary post of "presiding officer" of the JCS, a body consisting of the four chiefs of the four armed services, created as part of the new unified defense setup. When Ike heard talk that the temporary "presiding officer" position would likely be replaced by a longer-term chairman of the Joint Chiefs of Staff, he thought of Bradley—and, turning him down, Bradley, in turn, thought of General Joseph McNarney, a man who reveled in bureaucratic infighting. But when the post of chairman was formally created by Congress in 1949, McNarney proved to be a nonstarter because, as a U.S. Air Force general, his presence as chairman would have unfairly stacked air force representation (two generals) against navy representation (one admiral); nor did it seem appropriate to make an officer of a brand-new service arm the first JCS chairman. Asked to serve instead, Eisenhower flatly refused. And so the choice fell inevitably to Bradley.

Deeply concerned about the state of the American military establishment, he decided, this time, to accept.

It was a time of crisis. The air force had recently succeeded in diverting to itself funding earmarked for a navy supercarrier, touching off what would come to be called the "mutiny of the admirals," a revolt at the very top that Bradley feared could tear apart the Department of Defense, perhaps tempting the Soviets to take advantage of a perceived military disarray. Accustomed to dealing with such difficult personalities as Bernard Law Montgomery and George S. Patton Jr., Bradley believed that he might succeed as a moderating force that could prevent a damaging fight between the air force and navy. He was nevertheless deeply reluctant to step down as army chief, having served just a year and a half of the traditional four-year term as chief of staff and hardly satisfied with the progress he had made in "reshaping an administrative Army into a crack fighting force."[7] Nevertheless, the stakes were high, and Bradley was firmly committed to the successful unification of the military under the Department of Defense.

However determined he was to be an impartial mediator, Bradley soon concluded that the navy was indulging in a power grab, plain and simple. The immediate cause of the dispute was cancellation of funding for the planned navy supercarrier *America* in favor of funding nuclear-capable bombers, beginning with the B–36, for the air force. In congressional hearings, the navy charged that the military establishment, and therefore military budgeting, was devoted to a strategy of what Admiral Arthur Radford derisively called "atomic blitz." This, navy witnesses held, was a gravely misguided approach because atomic weapons would neither deter nor win a war; moreover, the admirals charged that such weapons were not only less powerful than advertised, but inherently immoral. Navy witnesses also criticized the air force's new bomber, the B–36, as vulnerable to attack and generally inadequate to its mission.

On the face of it, the navy made a powerful case, but Bradley believed that the admirals were engaging in self-serving dishonesty. The navy's assertion that the nation's military strategy was wholly dependent on atomic warfare was unfounded. As the navy well knew, Bradley and the JCS had been working on Project Offtackle, a program of mostly conventional (that is, non-nuclear) air, sea, and ground operations, in which the nuclear component was subordinate. And while Bradley agreed with the admirals that the ungainly, half-jet, half-piston-driven air force B–36 bomber was an imperfect weapon, he believed it was the best nuclear-capable aircraft available before the planned all-jet bombers, the B–47 Stratojet and the B–52 Stratofortress, would be ready to come online. Finally, Bradley was also convinced that the navy had cooked the books in its assessment of nuclear weapons, calling them less powerful than they actually were, and reaching a height of demagogical hypocrisy in criticizing them as immoral. Worst of all, Bradley deemed the navy's charges an "all-out assault on the credibility of our deterrent, our capability for waging nuclear war, [which] could completely undermine public trust both at home and abroad."[8]

His testimony to Congress was hard-hitting. Calling the Soviet surface fleet negligible, he claimed that it was wasteful to fund the U.S. Navy beyond what was needed to cope with the Soviet submarine threat. Additionally, because the U.S. Air Force had been assigned primary responsibility for strategic (nuclear) bombing, it was a mistake to fund supercarriers when the money was more urgently needed elsewhere. Moreover, the navy's claim that aircraft carriers would be needed to support future amphibious operations was unjustified because, Bradley predicted, large-scale amphibious operations would never occur again, thanks to the availability of the atomic bomb. Beyond his refutation of the navy's criticism of prevailing U.S. military strategy, Bradley had harsh words for navy leaders who had failed to learn the great lesson of World War II, that "our military forces are one team—in the game to win regardless who carries the ball." Continuing the metaphor born of his lifelong sports obsession, Bradley declared: "This is no time for 'fancy Dans' who won't hit the line with all they have on every play, unless they can call the signals. Each player on this team—whether he shines in the spotlight of the backfield or eats dirt in the line—must be all-American."[9]

Bradley's tough testimony made headlines, especially because it all came from an officer renowned for moderation of temper and temperament. In the end, the supercarrier *America* was not funded, while the B–36 was. Of more enduring significance was what Bradley's testimony revealed about the direction of American strategy during the early Cold War period. Although he was committed to developing the conventional warfare component of Offtackle, his testimony did reveal the depth of reliance American strategists were investing in strategic (nuclear) weapons. As for Bradley's prediction that amphibious warfare had become obsolete, it would be given the lie within little more than a year when, shortly after the outbreak of the Korean War, Douglas MacArthur led a spectacular amphibious assault at Inchon (September 15, 1950). In various "hot" encounters of the Cold War period—most importantly, in the Vietnam War—the American military's failure to fully develop its conventional tactical capabilities would have serious global strategic and political consequences. Bradley was by no means solely responsible for these strategic decisions, but he did support them and, with all their shortcomings, they guided American military planning and spending throughout most of the Cold War era.

+≈≈+

On April 4, 1949, representatives from Belgium, the Netherlands, Luxembourg, France, the United Kingdom, Canada, Portugal, Italy, Norway, Denmark, Iceland, and the United States gathered in Washington to sign the North Atlantic Treaty, creating the North Atlantic Treaty Organization (NATO), for the purpose of building a system of collective security, primarily against Soviet aggression. The signatories agreed (in Article V of the treaty) "that an armed attack against one or more of them . . . shall be considered an attack against them all." After the establishment of NATO, Joint Chiefs Chairman Bradley found himself with two additional duties. He chaired the NATO military committee, consisting of the chiefs of staff from all NATO nations, and he chaired a "standing group" within the military committee, analogous to the executive committee of a commercial board of directors, consisting of members from the United States, United Kingdom, and France. As a result his office became the epicenter of most of the free world's military policy making.

Bradley would serve at the top levels of NATO until he stepped down as chairman of the Joint Chiefs of Staff in August 1953. On September 20, 1950, the U. S. Congress recognized both his service in World

War II and his lofty stature in the postwar military establishment by authorizing his promotion to general of the army—a five-star general—belatedly putting him on a par with Marshall, MacArthur, Eisenhower, and Henry "Hap" Arnold, all of whom had been promoted to five-star rank during the war, in December 1944.

General of the Army Omar N. Bradley had little leisure to bask in his new rank, and NATO military committee chairman Bradley had little time to theorize about the course of the free world's military effort. His term as JCS chairman was soon engulfed by the Cold War period's first great hot war, which erupted in Korea on June 25, 1950 and which would not end until the uneasy 38th Parallel cease-fire on July 27, 1953.

The outbreak of the war caught Bradley at a time of illness; he was suffering from an unspecified "bug," apparently an intestinal infection, which caused significant fatigue and debility. Accepting the consensus of the Joint Chiefs, the ailing Bradley advised President Truman that the communist invasion of South Korea was in reality a diversion intended to draw Western attention away from the real communist objective, Formosa (Taiwan), the stronghold of Chiang Kai-shek's anti-Communist Nationalists. Bradley's assessment agreed with that of the American intelligence community, that is, that the Republic of Korea (ROK) Army— the army of South Korea—would ultimately prevail against the North Koreans. This assessment, Bradley later admitted, was based more on faith than on hard military intelligence. Despite both the feeling that Korea was a diversion and that the ROK Army, supplied with U.S. equipment and supported by the U.S. Air Force and U.S. Navy, would prevail, Bradley counseled that an American "failure to take action to protect South Korea would be appeasement and History proves that one appeasement leads to another and this inevitably leads to war." His advice—again reflecting JCS consensus—was to intervene, not so much to defend South Korea as such, but, in keeping with the Truman Doctrine, to oppose communist aggression. "We must draw the line somewhere," Bradley counseled, and Korea "offered as good an occasion for action in drawing the line as anywhere else."[10]

A nuanced combination of restraint and a call to action, Bradley's advice reflected what he later admitted was a simplistic belief virtually everyone held, that all Communist moves worldwide were the products of Stalin's monolithic direction.

+‌═══‌+

This view did not contemplate that the North Korean invasion might be, at least in part, the opening act in a local civil war, but held that it was necessarily a diversion—and not only from communist designs on nearby Formosa, but from communist designs on far-off Europe and the Middle East. Bradley and his colleagues speculated that Stalin had only temporarily set aside his plans for Europe and the Middle East in order to support a war fought by one of his Far Eastern satellites. Moreover, Korea might only be the first step in Far East. Formosa might be targeted next, and French Indochina (Vietnam) after that. The Philippines might also be in the Soviet crosshairs. Such thinking was the beginning of what journalists, a few years later, amplifying a remark by President Eisenhower, would dub the "domino theory." Diversion or not, let one small nation fall to Communism, and others—an entire region, even a large part of the world—would surely follow.

This was the climate of Cold War, the climate in which Bradley had to plan and manage his nation's meager military assets. Unlike any number of politicians, however, Bradley refused to partake in a panicky "Red scare." He did not believe that the Soviets were ready for anything like an expanded war. As Bradley saw it, Korea was chiefly a Soviet test of American resolve. Although the North Korean incursion suggested that Stalin was willing to take substantial provocative risks, Bradley initially opposed sending U.S. ground troops into Korea and advised instead restricting support to equipment and the employment of air and sea power.

In the meantime, however, Douglas MacArthur, commanding U.S. forces in the Far East, flew from his Tokyo headquarters to Korea and boldly drove up to the chaotic front lines of the communist incursion on June 29 to see the situation for himself. That night, he cabled Washington, calling for U.S. ground combat forces, one regimental combat team immediately, followed by two full divisions. Army chief of staff J. Lawton "Lightning Joe" Collins authorized ground forces to defend the strategic port of Pusan, but he told MacArthur that front-line deployment required a presidential decision. The always imperious MacArthur responded to the effect that there was no time for that, and Collins, ignoring and bypassing the JCS and Bradley, personally called Secretary of the Army Frank C. Pace, who in turn called Truman. The president authorized deployment of the combat team, and, a few hours later, deployment of the two divisions as well.

Bradley was persuaded that the commitment of ground troops was premature. Worse, without a war plan for Korea and with a limited post-war ground force, he believed that the United States was entering the war in the worst way—piecemeal. It was clear from the beginning that Bradley and the JCS would have remarkably little control over the conduct of the Korean War. "I only got to Korea twice during the fighting," Bradley admitted late in life. "Most of what I know about it is secondhand." The fact is that MacArthur improvised all planning and ran the war with a self-assumed autonomy far greater than what he had enjoyed in the Pacific theater of World War II and far beyond any authority that Eisenhower had exercised in that war's European theater. It is, of course, well known that President Truman, who never liked MacArthur, but who nevertheless appointed him supreme commander of UN forces in Korea, distrusted him deeply. Less widely known is that Bradley resented MacArthur even more strongly than Truman did. He and the JCS had grave misgivings about MacArthur's intention to invade Korea behind the enemy lines at Inchon. Indeed, there was a host of reasons not to attempt a landing at this place, with its treacherous tides and the high seawall behind the beach. Moreover, MacArthur was vague and evasive every time the Joint Chiefs asked for the details of his Inchon plan. That the operation turned out to be the tactical crown of MacArthur's military career, a spectacular triumph that—temporarily—turned the tables on the communist invaders, failed to impress Bradley, who mean-spiritedly dismissed Inchon as nothing more than "the luckiest military operation in history."[11]

Douglas MacArthur was an easy man not to like, and it was no secret in inner army circles that Omar Bradley did not like him. Nevertheless, as glibly unfair and unfounded as Bradley's denigration of the Inchon landing was, his resentment of MacArthur's egocentric approach to command cannot be dismissed as entirely personal. As chairman of the Joint Chiefs, he believed that MacArthur's self-centered orientation was hijacking U.S. military and political policy, focusing it entirely on Korea when, Bradley argued, the greatest danger remained Soviet aggression in Europe. The only way to restore the proper focus, Bradley reasoned, was to end the war in Korea as quickly as possible so that the troops could be at least partially redeployed to NATO in Europe. This meant pursuing a military policy that strictly limited the fighting to Korea and did not risk spreading it to communist China or the Soviet Union. Fighting China, Bradley famously cautioned, "would involve us in the wrong war, at the wrong place, at the wrong time, and with the wrong enemy."[12] As MacArthur's "no substitute for victory" posture became increasingly bellicose and expansionist, Bradley pushed back, adding to his global argument against tempting Chinese involvement a warning that MacArthur's fixation on Korea was leaving his first responsibility, occupied Japan, vulnerable to Soviet invasion. In the end, when Truman relieved an intractable and insubordinate MacArthur of UN supreme command on April 11, 1951, Bradley led the Joint Chiefs in unreserved support of the president's action. For him, MacArthur's removal did not represent the satisfaction of personal animosity, but had become a matter of national military necessity.

Bradley saw the Korean War to its ambiguous conclusion on July 27, 1953. Unlike MacArthur and most other military men, he harbored no bitterness over a failure to achieve total victory by reunifying the nation, but was satisfied that communism had been "contained" north of the 38th Parallel and that the war had not engulfed the region. Also in sharp contrast to most other military officers, Bradley retained an admiration for Harry S. Truman, and, although he was enormously relieved that Eisenhower, not MacArthur, had won the Republican nomination as presidential candidate in 1952, he was deeply disappointed by Eisenhower's embrace of such right-wing figures as Indiana's Senator William Jenner (who had vilified Marshall as a leftist "living lie") and Wisconsin's notorious Red-baiting Senator Joseph McCarthy.

After he stepped down as JCS chairman in August 1953, Bradley did not retire from the U.S. Army. By law, all five-star generals remained on the active list for life. Aside from occasional ceremonial duties, he had, however, withdrawn from military life. Almost immediately on leaving the JCS, he accepted a position with the Bulova Watch Company, first as head of its research and development laboratories and then, in 1958, on the death of Arde Bulova, as chairman of the company's board. Neither appointment was a sinecure. The aging Bradley worked vigorously and also sat on the boards of six other major firms. He did not retire from Bulova until 1973, at age eighty.

Omar Nelson Bradley lived 28 years after leaving the JCS. Following the death of his wife, Mary, from leukemia in 1965, he met Kitty Buhler, a 43-year-old, twice-divorced screenwriter, who interviewed Bradley in New York after she had acquired the rights to his life story. The two married on September 12, 1966, and the following year, the couple traveled to South Vietnam for a two-week tour of the combat zone. Together, they wrote an article on the war for *Look* magazine, in which Bradley concluded that this, at last, was "a war at the right place, at the right time and with the right enemy—the Communists."[13] He never apologized for— nor seemed to regret—this assessment.

In 1968, the Bradleys moved to Beverly Hills, California, where Kitty introduced her five-star husband to a galaxy of celebrities and facilitated a connection with film producer Frank McCarthy (who had been on General Marshall's World War II staff), who was at the time preparing production of what would be the classic film biography *Patton,* directed by Franklin Schaffner and starring George C. Scott. Kitty talked McCarthy into licensing Bradley's 1951 memoir *A Soldier's Story* as the basis for much of the movie's script and employing her husband as an advisor. The deal allowed the couple to transition from comfortably well-off to quite wealthy. Bradley endowed at West Point the Omar N. Bradley Library to house a portion of his papers, and he also funded Omar N. Bradley Fellowships in mathematics (his old West Point subject) and military history.

In late 1977, the Bradleys moved from Beverly Hills to quarters at Fort Bliss, El Paso, Texas, where the aging and increasingly infirm general could be given full-time medical care. On April 8, 1981, together with Kitty and a coterie of aides and medical corpsmen, Bradley was at New York City's 21 Club to accept the Gold Medal Award from the National

Institute of Social Sciences. Minutes after receiving the honor, as he was being wheeled into an elevator, eighty-eight-year-old Omar Bradley died. The cause was a blood clot in the brain, and his passing was as understated and dignified as his life and career had been—without convulsion, outcry, or even last words.

CHAPTER 14

Why Bradley Matters

Moments after receiving his penultimate public honor, Omar Nelson Bradley died. Six days later, President Ronald Reagan, recovering from John Hinckley's March 30 attempt on his life, ordered *Air Force One* to carry Kitty Bradley and her husband to Washington, where the General of the Army was buried with full military honors at Arlington National Cemetery.

No one, of course, questioned the rightness of the mode of transport or the burial honors. Bradley was a five-star American general, and many veterans and families of veterans who had served in World War II remembered him even more vividly as the "soldier's general" or the "GI General." Yet most Americans, in 1981, would have been hard-pressed to enumerate Bradley's military achievements. Even today, there are no pat answers to the question of why Bradley mattered in the history of World War II and why he continues to matter to the American military.

But he did matter, and he still does.

On July 26, 1940, in preparation for war, army chief of staff George C. Marshall and his staff established a General Headquarters (GHQ), analogous to what John J. Pershing had presided over during World War I. As Bradley observed, Marshall "had been stuck in a staff job against his will in World War I, but this time [as head of his own GHQ] he would command troops in the field, as a proper general should." Alas, Marshall's GHQ proved short-lived. "As the war expanded worldwide and the U.S. Army grew to millions upon millions of men, the quaint GHQ concept soon faded away," Bradley wrote.[1] With its passing, Marshall lost his chance to be a second Pershing. Instead, he became the first of a new breed of top commanders, whose duties were both produced and shaped by the mammoth and infinitely complex demands of World War II.

In earlier contests of arms, the supreme commanders were by necessity also the great captains, the leaders of troops in the field, inheritors of the mantle of Napoleon, Lee, and the like. But World War II was too big, its theaters and fronts too vast and far-flung, its alliances and enmities too numerous and too intricate for that. Great captains there were—the Rommels and the Pattons—but at the very top were the planners, the coordinators, and the administrators, men who occupied a gray region in which world and national politics uneasily mixed with considerations of the broadest military strategy, thorny issues of field commanders' jarring egos and varying abilities, and the hard, unglamorous nitty-gritty of logistics. Marshall was one of this new breed, as were the men who became his chief lieutenants, Dwight David Eisenhower and Omar Nelson Bradley.

Put most simply, Marshall ran the United States Army in World War II, inhabiting a layer of command and administration between the president and Congress on the one hand and the theater commanders on the other. Ike Eisenhower ran the Allied armies in the European Theater of Operations, working between the political war leaders (FDR, Winston Churchill, and, to some extent, Charles de Gaulle) and the commanders who led the field forces. Military historians and even the public have come to understand and to appreciate the roles these two men played. Bradley's role, however, was both richer and more ambiguous.

In contrast to both Marshall and Eisenhower, neither of whom had ever held a combat command, Bradley did lead in combat a corps and then an army and, finally, a vast army group of 1.3 million men. His rise in World War II was from observer-advisor in North Africa, to Patton's "understudy" in II Corps, to commander of II Corps, to commander of First U.S. Army and First U.S. Army Group, to commander of Twelfth U.S. Army Group (the largest single field command in American military history), to co-architect—some even believe de facto primary architect—of the endgame strategy of the European campaign.

Like Marshall and Ike, Bradley became a new kind of officer: a military executive, whose planning and management responsibilities straddled the military and political realms. Born in the exigencies of World War II, this new breed of commander would become even more important during the Cold War era that followed as well as the epoch of nation building—from the war-torn Balkans to the war-torn Middle East—that succeeded the Cold War. Each of the top American generals provided a model for the new demands that would be made on postwar military leadership, but, more than either Eisenhower or Marshall, Bradley showed how an "ordinary" line officer could rise productively to the highest level.

The careers of Marshall, Eisenhower, and Bradley were more similar than they were different; for none of the three had held combat commands before World War II. Marshall had served in France during World War I, but his service was on Pershing's staff and not in the field. Neither Eisenhower nor Bradley had even been sent overseas. But whereas Marshall and Eisenhower would lead no combat troops in World War II, Bradley did, and that made his experience richer than that of either of his seniors. Moreover, in the years leading up to World War II, Bradley not only studied at all the army professional schools, he taught at all levels, as an ROTC instructor at South Dakota State College, as an instructor at West Point, and as an instructor at the Infantry School. Later, he was a tactical officer at West Point—one of a small cadre charged, in effect, with teaching cadets the essentials of being soldier-officers—and, in the early months of the war, he was commandant of the Infantry School, directing the training of the junior officers who would lead the victory in World War II.

Perhaps Bradley's single most important contribution to army training beginning in the World War II era was the creation of the Officer Candidate School (OCS) concept, which he instituted at the Infantry

School and which soon spread throughout the army. West Point and college ROTC programs could not be counted on to produce a sufficient number of adequately trained officers to meet the demands of world war, and existing National Guard officers tended to be poorly trained and inept, while Reserve officers were simply too old. Bradley gave the army a means of selecting men from the enlisted ranks, including brand-new inductees, and transforming them into competent junior officers. The OCS system remains a vital component of the American military today, providing the majority of officers in all of the service branches.

Beyond the specific achievement of OCS, Bradley instilled in a generation of junior officers—those who fought in World War II, in Korea, in Vietnam, and into the conflicts of the present day—four key war-fighting precepts:

1. Understanding terrain—the battlespace—in all of its dimensions, not just on a flat map.
2. Seeing all aspects of a battle from the point of view of the enemy.
3. The unglamorous art and science of logistics.
4. The importance—the supreme importance—of the individual soldier.

Most of today's most advanced military technology is devoted to realistically modeling the battlespace. Bradley was at work on this effort long before the advent of computers and artificial intelligence software.

Likewise, a very large part of military intelligence—and general political intelligence—is today devoted to getting inside the mind of the enemy or potential enemies. Bradley made this a top priority, both on a literal battlefield level—What does the enemy *see?*—and on a more abstract intellectual and psychological level: What *motivates* the enemy?

Bradley was one of a select cadre of far-seeing officers who embraced the doctrine of "open warfare"—of maximum mobility—but, in contrast to those (like Patton) who conceived of mechanized warfare mainly in terms of rapid assault, Bradley put the emphasis on creating the logistical means of sustaining open warfare. To be sure, this was the unglamorous side of rapid military movement, but today's military is first and foremost a logistical enterprise. Bradley was instrumental in shifting military strategy to a focus on engineering the best possible systems of supply, transport, and sustenance.

It is, however, in connection with the fourth point—the focus on the individual soldier—that Omar Bradley is most widely remembered and most obviously linked to the modern military. Iconoclasts have asserted that his reputation as the "soldier's general" or the "GI General" was wholly the invention of World War II's most popular field correspondent, Ernie Pyle. There is no denying that Pyle admired Bradley and gave him a great deal of publicity, portraying him as a democratic foil to the "Prussian" autocracy embodied in Patton. Yet it was no mere fabrication. Bradley grew from the humblest of roots. Although, as a professional soldier, he endeavored to remain apolitical, his lifelong political sympathies were Populist, always favoring the "ordinary Joe" and the "little guy." He believed that soldiers should be well-disciplined but also well-treated, treated with respect as citizens first and as soldiers second. Concerned about the demoralizing impact mass conscription was having on new draftees in World War II, he instituted procedures to make incoming recruits feel they were being given a new home and that they were also becoming part of an elite force in the noblest of causes. Bradley's approach prompted some critics to accuse him of "coddling" the troops, but it nevertheless became a model universally adopted throughout the army and is today reflected in the military's emphasis on the individual soldier as an *individual* first and foremost. Bradley's emphasis on developing the individual to his fullest potential presaged the orientation of today's army, whose recent recruiting slogans have included the imperatives to "Be all that you can be" and to "Be an army of one."

+⇒⋅⇐+

As we saw in Chapter 11, the Battle of the Bulge was a blow to Bradley's prestige and for a time threatened his standing as an army group commander. His recovery during this battle and his synergistic working relationship with General Patton not only rehabilitated his reputation, but put him in position to preside over the Rhine crossings that were the climax of the European campaign. The success of the Twelfth Army Group in forcing the crossings and then exploiting them catapulted Bradley into

Ike Eisenhower's inner circle. It was in the final phase of the European war that he was at last given the opportunity to draw up strategy on a large scale.

He did so boldly and with nothing but military considerations in view. Bradley had the courage to tell Eisenhower that Berlin was not worth the cost of winning. He confirmed Ike in his over-riding plan to kill the enemy army rather than invest men and equipment in taking "political" and "prestige" objectives. The decision to leave Berlin to the Soviets, a decision identified with Bradley as much as with Eisenhower, created great controversy and certainly had a profound effect on postwar geopolitics. The choice remains starkly relevant today as an object lesson in military decision making, the weighing of political versus military objectives, and the difficult necessity of reaching a decision that is not unduly deformed by political and popular pressure. Bradley would face this dilemma again during the Korean War, when he struggled to maintain the national military focus on what he saw as the worldwide threats of Communist aggression at a time when small and distant Korea was the blinding mote in the eye of virtually all American politicians and military leaders.

During the endgame of World War II and the Korean War phase of the Cold War, Bradley was compelled to invent himself as a global strategist. The U.S. Army War College he had attended taught strategy in the traditional narrow military sense of the word—essentially as the manipulation of armies and the military management of theaters of war. After Bradley, the War College broadened its approach to strategy that now united military, geopolitical, and economic considerations. It is now assumed that all top commanders will do what Bradley had to do—not only lead armies, but lead them within an increasingly complex geopolitical and economic context.

✦═══✦

Following World War II, after unglamorous but demanding and important service as head of the Veterans Administration (VA), during which he transformed the VA medical service into the world's premier healthcare system for military veterans, Bradley became U.S. Army chief of staff, the first chairman of the Joint Chiefs of Staff, and head of the military committee and "standing group" of the military committee of the newly created North Atlantic Treaty Organization (NATO).

With these lofty assignments, Omar Bradley became America's top Cold War general. Yet he discovered that the army's senior commander had but limited power in the postwar world. Bradley had to shift from commanding massive forces in total war to parceling out much smaller forces to fight limited wars, actions intended to "contain" the aggressive spread of Communism without igniting larger, regional wars or even a third world war.

Bradley was America's first manager of the limited war concept. He was also the first coordinator of an ongoing, institutionalized alliance, NATO, directed almost exclusively against a single, specific threat, the Soviet Union and its satellites. Additionally, he was expected to manage the unification of four service branches—army, navy, marines, and the newly independent U.S. Air Force—each of which had many conflicting demands and needs. Perhaps most difficult of all, Bradley presided over the senior officers of a military establishment that now had a growing nuclear capability. He had to anticipate the war-fighting needs of the post–World War II era and balance the strategic (that is, nuclear) deterrent against tactical (nonnuclear) forces. His championing of Project Off-tackle represented the core of this attempt—to create a kind of military continuum encompassing a flexible conventional capability as well as a strong nuclear deterrent.

Did Bradley achieve the balance he sought? Based on the American experience in Korea and Vietnam, he did not. But he identified the problem, and he made a start toward solving it, placing it foremost on the agendas of the senior military commanders who succeeded him. The collapse of Soviet-based communism in the early 1990s has drawn America's military focus away from nuclear deterrence even as the rise of non-state threats—especially those posed by militant religious extremist groups—has directed that focus ever more intensely on further developing conventional capability. Yet even in the midst of the Cold War era, with its emphasis on strategic weapons, Bradley worked within often draconian budget constraints to maintain and even improve the army's conventional capabilities. At the very least, he kept the issue of conventional war-fighting capability before Congress and his military colleagues.

━━━

Continuum. The word has special relevance as a description of the military legacy of Omar Bradley. From the beginning of his career, he conceived of the ideal officer as possessing a continuum of qualities—basic soldiering skills, high regard for the individual soldier, complete technical mastery of the profession of arms, tactical and strategic vision, unimpeachable moral character, dauntless courage, and a great capacity for leadership—just as, at the end of his career, he sought to create a military structure in which the four service branches and their range of weapons systems existed seamlessly enough to give the nation's civilian and military leaders a continuum of options for successfully coping with the threats of Cold War, hot war, and even total war. Much of Bradley's military career had unfolded between the world wars, when the army was treated by politicians and public alike as a kind of unwanted appendage on democratic society. By the closing months of World War II in Europe and in the early years of the Cold War Bradley labored to ensure that the American military would become integral to American political life and part of diplomatic continuum. The postwar world demanded nothing less.

In none of these profound undertakings was Omar Bradley a dramatic, mercurial, or colorful presence. The threats and issues he faced were bigger than life, but he never was. And he never wanted to be. Everything Bradley did was rooted in the values of his Missouri childhood, youth, and young manhood: values of common sense, Populist patriotism, basic decency, a commitment to hard work, a willingness to learn, a desire to teach, and a quiet, unassuming, selfless passion to serve.

Endnotes

Introduction

1. Harry C. Butcher, *My Three Years with Eisenhower—1942–1945* (New York: Simon and Schuster, 1946), p. 298; Omar N. Bradley with Clay Blair, *A General's Life* (New York: Simon and Schuster, 1983), p. 200.
2. See Charles Whiting, *Bradley* (New York: Ballantine Books, 1971), *passim*.

Chapter 1

1. Omar N. Bradley with Clay Blair, *A General's Life* (New York: Simon and Schuster, 1983), p. 18.
2. Bradley, Ibid., p. 17.
3. Bradley, Ibid., p. 18.
4. Bradley, Ibid., pp 18–19.
5. Bradley, Ibid., p. 19.
6. Bradley, Ibid.
7. Bradley, Ibid., pp. 22, 23.
8. Bradley, Ibid., p. 24.
9. Bradley, Ibid.
10. Bradley, Ibid., p. 25.
11. Bradley, Ibid.
12. Bradley, Ibid., p. 26.

Chapter 2

1. Omar N. Bradley with Clay Blair, *A General's Life* (New York: Simon and Schuster, 1983), p. 27.
2. Bradley, Ibid., p. 28.
3. Bradley, Ibid.

4. Bradley, Ibid., pp. 30–31, 32.
5. Bradley, Ibid., pp. 31, 32.
6. Bradley, Ibid., p. 34.
7. Bradley, Ibid., p. 35.

Chapter 3

1. Omar N. Bradley with Clay Blair, *A General's Life* (New York: Simon and Schuster, 1983), p. 35; United States Military Academy, *The Howitzer* (New York: The Hoskins Press, 1915), p. 55.
2. United States Military Academy, *The Howitzer,* p. 55.
3. Bradley, *A General's Life,* p. 36.
4. Ibid., pp. 36–37.
5. Ibid., p. 37.
6. Ibid., p. 38.
7. Ibid., p. 41; for more on "motorized hikes" and Eisenhower and the transcontinental convoy, see Carlo d'Este, *Eisenhower: A Soldier's Life* (New York: Henry Holt, 2002), pp. 140–144.
8. Bradley, *A General's Life,* p. 44.
9. Ibid., pp. 44–45.
10. Ibid., p. 46.

Chapter 4

1. Omar N. Bradley with Clay Blair, *A General's Life* (New York: Simon and Schuster, 1983), p. 51.
2. Ibid., p. 51.
3. Ibid., p. 54.
4. Ibid., p. 58.
5. Ibid., p. 59.
6. Ibid., p. 60.
7. Ibid., p. 61.

Chapter 5

1. Omar N. Bradley with Clay Blair, *A General's Life* (New York: Simon and Schuster, 1983), p. 63.
2. Ibid., p. 62.
3. Ed Cray, *General of the Army: George C. Marshall, Soldier and Statesman* (reprint ed., New York: Cooper Square Press, 2000), p. 105.
4. Cray, *General of the Army,* p. 105.
5. Bradley, *A General's Life,* p. 64; Cray, *General of the Army,* pp. 105–106.
6. Bradley quoted in Cray, *General of the Army,* p. 106.
7. Bradley, *A General's Life,* p. 65.
8. Ibid., pp. 65–66.
9. Ibid., p. 66.

10. Clay Blair, interview with Matthew Ridgway, quoted in Bradley, *A General's Life*, p. 66.

11. Bradley, *A General's Life*, p. 68.

12. Ibid., p. 69.

13. Ibid., p.71.

Chapter 6

1. Omar N. Bradley with Clay Blair, *A General's Life* (New York: Simon and Schuster, 1983), p. 76.

2. William C. Westmoreland, *A Soldier Remembers* (Garden City, N.Y.: Doubleday, 1976), p. 134.

3. Westmoreland, *A Soldier Remembers*, p. 134.

4. Bradley, *A General's Life*, pp. 77–78.

5. George C. Marshall to Bradley, quoted in Bradley, *A General's Life*, p. 78.

6. Bradley, *A General's Life*, p. 79.

7. Ibid., p. 83.

8. Ibid., p. 84.

9. Ibid.

10. Ibid., p. 85.

11. Ibid.

12. Ibid.

13. Ibid., p. 88.

14. Winston S. Churchill, *Their Finest Hour* (reprint ed., Boston: Houghton Mifflin, 1985), p. 22.

15. Bradley, *A General's Life*, p. 93.

16. Ibid., p. 93.

17. Ibid., p. 94.

18. Ibid., p. 96.

19. Ibid., pp. 99, 98.

20. Ibid., p. 100.

21. Patton, letter to Bradley, February 18, 1942, in Martin Blumenson, comp. and ed., *The Patton Papers 1940–1945* (reprint ed., New York: Da Capo, 1996), p. 55.

22. Bradley, *A General's Life*, p. 102.

23. Ibid., p. 102.

Chapter 7

1. Omar N. Bradley with Clay Blair, *A General's Life* (New York: Simon and Schuster, 1983), p. 106.

2. Ibid., p. 106. Looking to build morale "in every possible way," Bradley invited Sergeant Alvin C. York to talk to the men of his old outfit. "Sergeant York's visit was a tremendous morale builder for the troops," Bradley later wrote. "But he surely deflated me. On his departure he told me in his candid hill-country way that I would not get very far in this world because I was 'too nice.'" (Ibid., p. 107.)

3. Ibid., pp. 106, 107.

4. Ibid., p. 110.
5. The following exchange is quoted from ibid., p. 113.
6. Ibid., p. 131.
7. Eisenhower to Marshall, February 11, 1943, in Alfred D. Chandler, Jr., ed., *The Papers of Dwight David Eisenhower: The War Years II* (Baltimore: The Johns Hopkins Press, 1970), p. 951.
8. Bradley, *A General's Life,* p. 132.
9. Ibid., p. 133.
10. Ibid., p. 135. In his *Patton: A Genius for War* (New York: HarperCollins, 1995), Carlo d'Este describes Lloyd Fredendall as "dour and imperious" (p. 388); d'Este quotes Major General Ernest Harmon's assessment: "a son-of-a-bitch" (p. 460). British general Harold Alexander stunned Eisenhower by remarking of Fredendall, "I'm sure you must have better men than that" (p. 460). Patton relieved Fredendall as II Corps commander on March 6, 1943, and Fredendall spent the rest of the war in Stateside training missions.
11. Harmon's remark to Patton quoted in Carlo d'Este, *Patton,* p. 460.
12. The following exchange is quoted in Bradley, *A General's Life,* p. 137.
13. Ibid., p. 139. Patton voiced great disdain for foxholes and slit trenches, which he thought inherently cowardly. Bradley was shocked when Patton, touring the 1st Division encampment of Terry de la Mesa Allen, surveyed the slit trenches and approached Allen. "Terry, which one is yours?" Patton asked. Allen pointed to his slit trench. "Patton strode over, unzipped his fly and urinated into the trench. Imperiously rezipping his fly, Patton sneered at Terry: "Now try to use it." (Ibid., p. 140.)
14. Ibid., p. 142.
15. Ibid., p. 145.
16. Patton, letter to Bradley, April 23, 1943, in Martin Blumenson, comp. and ed., *The Patton Papers 1940–1945* (reprint ed., New York: Da Capo, 1996), p. 232; Bradley, *A General's Life,* p. 151.

Chapter 8

1. Omar N. Bradley with Clay Blair, *A General's Life* (New York: Simon and Schuster, 1983), p. 154.
2. Ibid., p. 156.
3. Ibid.
4. Ibid., p. 157.
5. Ibid., p. 159.
6. Ibid., p. 163.
7. Ibid., pp. 171–172; Bradley, letter to Marshall, May 29, 1943, quoted in ibid., p. 172.
8. Bradley, *A General's Life,* p. 189.
9. For a full discussion of the Patton "slapping incidents," see Alan Axelrod, *Patton* (New York: Palgrave Macmillan, 2006), pp. 113–122. Initially, Bradley was made aware only of the second incident, which he took steps to cover up, concerned lest "we . . . lose Patton's talents forever." (Bradley, *A General's Life,* p. 198)
10. Bradley, *A General's Life,* p. 200.

Chapter 9

1. For Patton on Mark W. Clark, see Martin Blumenson, comp. and ed., *The Patton Papers 1940–1945* (reprint ed., New York: Da Capo, 1996), pp. 84, 87, and 138.
2. Eisenhower, letter to Marshall, August 27, 1943, in Alfred D. Chandler, Jr., ed., *The Papers of Dwight David Eisenhower: The War Years: II* (Baltimore: The Johns Hopkins Press, 1970), pp. 1357–1358.
3. Eisenhower, letter to Marshall, August 28, 1943, in Chandler, ed., *The Papers of Dwight David Eisenhower,* p. 1364.
4. Marshall, letter to Eisenhower, September 1, 1943, quoted in Omar N. Bradley with Clay Blair, *A General's Life* (New York: Simon and Schuster, 1983), p. 205; Bradley, *A General's Life,* p. 207.
5. Bradley, *A General's Life,* pp. 210, 211.
6. Ibid., p. 212.
7. Patton's remarks to the Knutsford Welcome Club, April 25, 1944, are found in Blumenson, comp. and ed., *The Patton Papers 1940–1945,* pp. 440–441.
8. Bradley quoted in J. Lawton Collins, *Lightning Joe: An Autobiography* (reprint ed., Novato, Calif.: Presidio Press, 1994), p. 180.
9. Eisenhower's remark is quoted in Harry C. Butcher, *My Three Years with Eisenhower—1942–1945* (New York: Simon and Schuster, 1946), p. 434.
10. Bradley, *A General's Life,* p. 235.
11. Ibid., p. 242.
12. Maxwell D. Taylor, *Swords and Plowshares: A Memoir* (reprint ed., New York: Da Capo, 2001), p. 747.
13. Bradley, *A General's Life,* p. 244.
14. Ibid., p. 244.
15. Ibid., p. 251.

Chapter 10

1. Like other American commanders, Bradley can be faulted for not adopting any of "Hobart's funnies," a set of ingenious armored vehicles specially adapted for breaching obstacles—including hedgerows—by engineers of Major General Sir Percy Hobart's British 79th Armored Division. Bradley (and other American officers) considered Hobart's innovations too outlandish.
2. Charles Whiting, *Bradley* (New York: Ballantine, 1971), p. 26.
3. Patton, diary, July 23, 1944, in Martin Blumenson, comp. and ed., *The Patton Papers 1940–1945* (reprint ed., New York: Da Capo, 1996), p. 486.
4. The launch of Operation Cobra is detailed in Omar Bradley, *A Soldier's Story* (reprint ed., New York: Modern Library, 1999), p. 348.
5. Patton, letter to Eisenhower, July 28, 1944, and diary entry, July 1944, in Blumenson, comp. and ed., *The Patton Papers 1940–1945,* pp. 489, 491.
6. Whiting, *Bradley,* p. 31.
7. Omar N. Bradley with Clay Blair, *A General's Life* (New York: Simon and Schuster, 1983), p. 363.
8. Ibid.

9. Ibid.
10. Ibid.

Chapter 11

1. Omar N. Bradley with Clay Blair, *A General's Life* (New York: Simon and Schuster, 1983), p. 299.
2. Patton, letter to his son George S. Patton IV, September 17, 1944, and diary entry, September 17, 1944, in Martin Blumenson, comp. and ed., *The Patton Papers 1940–1945* (reprint ed., New York: Da Capo, 1996), p. 550.
3. Bradley, *A General's Life*, p. 351.
4. Ibid., p. 356; Patton, diary, December 16, 1944, in Blumenson, comp. and ed., *The Patton Papers 1940–1945*, p. 595.
5. Bradley, *A General's Life*, p. 357.
6. Dwight David Eisenhower, *Crusade in Europe* (reprint ed., Baltimore: The Johns Hopkins Press, 1997), p. 350.
7. Carlo d'Este, *Patton: A Genius for War* (New York: HarperCollins, 1995), p. 680.
8. Bradley, *A General's Life*, pp. 363–364.
9. This exchange between Bradley and Eisenhower is reported in Geoffrey Perret, *Eisenhower* (Avon, Mass.: Adams Media, 1999), p. 331.
10. Bradley, *A General's Life*, p. 368.

Chapter 12

1. Montgomery quoted in Arthur Bryant, *Triumph in the West: A History of the War Years Based on the Diaries of Field-Marshal Lord Alanbrooke, Chief of the Imperial General Staff* (reprint ed., Westport, Conn.: Greenwood Press, 1974), p. 278.
2. Omar N. Bradley with Clay Blair, *A General's Life* (New York: Simon and Schuster, 1983), p. 371.
3. Ibid.; Patton, diary, December 27, 1944, in Martin Blumenson, comp. and ed., *The Patton Papers 1940–1945* (reprint ed., New York: Da Capo, 1996), p. 608.
4. Bradley, *A General's Life*, p. 372.
5. Marshall, letter to Eisenhower, quoted in ibid., p. 376.
6. Ralph Ingersoll, *Top Secret* (New York: Harcourt, Brace, 1946), p. 279; Bradley, *A General's Life*, p. 383; Omar Bradley, *A Soldier's Story* (reprint ed., New York: Modern Library, 1999), p. 488.
7. Bradley, *A General's Life*, pp. 383–384.
8. Ibid., pp. 405–406.
9. Ibid., p. 407.
10. Ibid.
11. Ibid.
12. Patton, diary, March 9, 1945, in Blumenson, comp. and ed., *The Patton Papers 1940–1945*, p. 653.
13. James M. Gavin, *On to Berlin: Battles of an Airborne Commander 1943–1946* (reprint ed., New York: Bantam, 1984), pp. 306–307; Bradley, *A General's Life*, p. 416.
14. Bradley, *A Soldier's Story*, pp. 535, 534.

15. Charles Whiting, *Bradley* (New York: Ballantine, 1971), p. 115.
16. Bradley, *A General's Life*, p. 436.
17. Ibid.
18. Ibid.

Chapter 13

1. Omar N. Bradley with Clay Blair, *A General's Life* (New York: Simon and Schuster, 1983), p. 435; Eisenhower, letter to Marshall, April 26, 1945, in Alfred D. Chandler, Jr., ed., *The Papers of Dwight David Eisenhower: The War Years: IV* (Baltimore: The Johns Hopkins Press, 1970), pp. 2647–2648.
2. Marshall, letter to Eisenhower, April 27, 1945, quoted in Bradley, *A General's Life*, p. 435; Bradley, *A General's Life*, p. 439.
3. Ibid., p. 440.
4. Ibid., p. 446.
5. Miller and Monhan's *Reader's Digest* article quoted in Bradley, *A General's Life*, p. 461; Bradley, *A General's Life*, p. 462.
6. Ibid., p. 498.
7. Ibid., p. 505.
8. Ibid., pp. 508, 509.
9. Ibid., p. 511.
10. Ibid., pp. 537, 534, 535.
11. Ibid., pp. 539–540, 541, 556.
12. Bradley's full assessment of the dangers of expanding the Korean War are found in Barton J. Bernstein and Allen J. Matusow, eds., *The Truman Administration: A Documentary History* (reprint ed., New York: Harper Colophon, 1968), pp. 476–481.
13. The *Look* magazine article (November 14, 1967) is quoted in Bradley, *A General's Life*, p. 677.

Chapter 14

1. Omar N. Bradley with Clay Blair, *A General's Life* (New York: Simon and Schuster, 1983), p. 92.

Index